PRAISE FOR

WARRIOR DANCE

"*Warrior Dance* paints a beautiful picture of fierce triumph over trials. PJ Clark has laid it all out; her life; her struggles; and her strategies for overcoming. She takes us on her journey and shows us how we, too, can find victory. We've been friends for many years. PJ's intimate relationship with the Father is so evident. Her strength is in her passion and ability to release us all into joyous freedom. This book has the potential to set us back on the course God planned for us since before time. It's time. The world needs your gift."

Chris Tracy

Author, Blogger, Writing Coach - www.christinetracy.com
Leader in Create Academy - www.theresadedmon.com

"Are you ready to access your Warrior within? Do you want to move forward into the glorious promises God has given you? PJ Clark, in *Warrior Dance*, will help you discover your calling and gain courage to step out of your comfort zone to discover the Warrior whom God created you to be. In her book, PJ is vulnerable, sharing her story of her desire to be the Warrior that God created her to be. PJ shares the "lies" and then the 'tactics' of how you can run your race with courage and see what God can do for you. Trust PJ when she offers her encouraging advice in *Warrior Dance*."

Earl Menchhofer

Author, *Stay in the Game - 7 Steps to Serenity*

"Join PJ as she helps you delve deeper into your heart by sharing her life story, original poetry, and art. She also includes thought-provoking questions and gives tips on how to enter into your own healing art journey. Add this book to your arsenal of weapons to destroy any hidden darkness in your life and bring the light and truth to others. Join the Army of the Warrior Bride!"

Iris D. Armstrong
Art and Dance Warrior
Banners of Love

"Have you ever felt unseen, disassociated from your destiny and calling and you don't know where to start? Look no further! PJ Clark in the *Warrior Dance* gives you steps and tools to reconnect, reconcile, and reclaim your destiny and reignite desires you thought were lost and forgotten. Where you feel undesirable, God has given PJ the tools and knowledge to empower you to move from the darkness and into the light and step into your calling as a child of God. May you be blessed with the knowledge and grace that flows from *Warrior Dance!*"

Abigayle Nunez
Reverent Rhythms Professional Dance Company and School of the Arts
Assistant Director, Company Dancer

"PJ has captured the essence of deepening intimacy with Jesus in worship through dance and flagging. In *Warrior Dance*, the Lord will teach you the beauty of incorporating this form of worship in your quiet times with Him. PJ's teaching on journaling your impressions of the Lord's words to you will enrich your walk with the Lord and bring inner healing in amazing ways. There are many nuggets and nuances in *Warrior Dance* that will cause you to stop and ponder; will create desire in your heart to bring new forms of worship into your life."

Beverly Gadbois
Aglow State Prayer Coordinator for Colorado

"P.J. is a woman of faith, full of creativity and art. Her story paints a beautiful picture of how God, the Ultimate Warrior, calls us together in a Warrior Dance journey to freedom. Although her life was wrought with obstacles and entanglements, with the help of 'The One,' she resisted and pushed back the darkness, never giving up or surrendering. *Warrior Dance* is her invitation to us to join the dance and find grace, peace, and victory with each step we take. An inspiration and joy, I am honored to call her a friend and shining star.... bold, brave, and beautiful."

Lonnette Kelley
Author and Speaker
www.Joyintheheartland.com

"PJ takes you on a beautifully raw and intimate journey, a relentless and courageous pursuit, to unearth what she calls her *Warrior Dance*. Walk along with her as she shows you how to uncover beauty from ashes, shine light in the dark places, and experience unrivaled freedom from the captivity so often found in oneself. A relatable and interactive guide that will push you to discover and put into practice your very own *Warrior Dance*."

Lindsay Blaszak
Nutritional Therapy Practitioner (February 2023)

"PJ is a worshiping Warrior in the Kingdom of God who introduced me to the 'surrendered life' of Galatians 2:20 thirty-three years ago when our children were small, and we were young wives and mothers. As we became passionate lovers of Jesus (we who had been forgiven much, loved much [Luke 7:36-50]), we learned to dance with abandon before our Redeemer and Lord, Jesus, and we learned to 'war' together in spiritual battles with praises and the sword of the Word resounding from our lips."

Harriet Cash
Chattanooga Realty
Worshiper of the Most High King

"PJ writes a deep, thought-provoking story of her life. Through her transparent and vulnerable journey, she shares her difficult and dark moments. She writes how God met her each step of the way…how He rescued, led her, and opened up healing through the Word. Through her gift of the arts, God empowered her to understand His Warrior Spirit. Her passion is inspiring, challenging, and moving. Not a read to rush through, this book will encourage and challenge you to get beneath the surface of your life, to dig deep into your belief system, and realize and walk in your power and authority to emerge as a mighty Warrior of God."

Angie Taylor

Realtor, Investor, Consultant, Builder, Designer
United Country Real Colorado Properties

"Through her willingness to be vulnerable and share from the depths of her heart, PJ gives us a glimpse of the twists and turns she encountered as she navigated her life's journey with God by her side. Her ability to be real as she shares her fears, pains, joys, and transformation gives us hope and inspiration that we, too, can lower our walls to face our own battles as we discover and embrace the Warrior in each one of us."

Dr. Myra Heckenlaible-Gotto, EdD

*Author of Crossing Life's Bridges: Navigating Transitions
and Creating Shifts. . .Bit by Bit*

"Like a precious, gold locket, hidden inside the heart of God, the brave writer, author, and creator of *Warrior Dance* has been set free to ignite a generation of creative worshippers in spirit and in truth! PJ Clark poignantly touches on all 'humanity's heart cry,' to know and be known."

Gloria L. Sutter

*Author, Illustrator, Song Writer of Wingless Bird-Like a Bird, You are Heard
Creator of "Dear Globug Books, a Children's Ministry Book Series"
www.dearglobug.com*

"Many years ago, I prayed for a spiritual friend who was as hungry as I was to know God and His peace. He gave me PJ. The things we learned during our season together are deeply woven into the person I am now. This is a wonderful book. PJ's authenticity, heart, and wisdom shine throughout. It is not an easy thing to condense a lifetime of learning and wisdom into a book, but PJ has done it. She has taken all the trials, tribulations, and funny side roads we took seeking God and cut right to the chase to show people how to be healed and free. Well done, dear friend. Creation waits for the revealing of the sons and daughters of God."

Karen B. Miller
Artist and Photographer

WARRIOR
DANCE

TABLE OF CONTENTS

PART ONE: WARRIOR DEFINED AND FREEDOM FROM WHAT?

PART TWO: DARK CLOUDS AND DEEP PITS

PART THREE: DISCOVERING YOUR VOICE
THROUGH THE ARTS

PART FOUR: ACTIVATE THE WARRIOR WITHIN

PART FIVE: CONCLUSION

DEDICATION

To my husband Mike, my "earthly rock" who has stayed by my side through the *dark clouds and deep pits of life*, and journeyed with me on the high vistas of *splendor and glory*. It was in the magnificent Colorado Rocky Mountains that our hearts first met. We have lived life to the fullest! Blessed with three remarkable children, their families and seven "Grand Warriors" as our legacy of faith, family, and love continues. I will be forever grateful for your undying patience, unconditional love, and full acceptance of me. Without our prevailing faith and love of God, this book wouldn't have been possible. You are my Brave Warrior. ONWARD!

FOREWORD

It's time to find your sword and learn to fight with the arsenal God has given you in the creative realm where Heaven meets Earth within us.

In the book, *Warrior Dance*, you will discover how to war against the enemy through God's presence, His Word, journaling, dancing, creating art, and listening to your heart.

As a creative forerunner, I have seen so many people live below what God has destined for them because they don't know how to fight defeating mindsets or set goals for themselves. They have never learned to let God into the pain of their stories. So many try to travel the road of life on their own, instead of linking arms with others around them who can help lift them up and give them the courage they need.

You don't have to do it alone! When you read about PJ's story, relate it to your own life journey, while she practically leads you to find the Warrior that may be hiding within you.

Throughout each section, she shares her journey through poetry, great movies, and her search for meaning and freedom.

We all need to remember that great Warriors like William Wallace, Joan of Arc, and Mother

Teresa all had many small choices along the way that prepared them for their ultimate fight with slavery, political tyranny, and poverty. The power of overcoming so many great obstacles within their journey for the freedom of others was a result of thousands of choices they made in their lives prior to the great victories that made them icons of Warriors on a worldwide scale.

We must start with where we are right now and enter into the story of how our lives are intrinsically intertwined with God. Ephesians 1:4 in The Passion Translation says, "And he (God) chose us to be his very own, joining us to himself even before he laid the foundations of the universe!"

It all starts with yielding to God and learning who we are. Our first yes to God is built upon the choices we make daily that no one sees except the One who formed us. Each yes conforms us to understand God's battle plan for our lives and how to use the weapons of our warfare.

In raising up countless creatives around the world, I am in the company of so many Warriors who are learning not to shrink back from believing they are joined to the Creator God in a splendid story, where they can be raised up to be Warriors, fighting for His Kingdom.

At my Create Academy, I have had the awesome privilege of mentoring PJ who is raising up so many other creatives to war for their destiny through art, dance, and prophetic ministry. This book has been written through tears, joy, laughter, and covenant friendships.

Now, it's your turn. Discover the Warrior within, take up your sword, fight with your comrades, and win each battle, small or large, in honor of the King!

As a spiritual mother, I bless you on your creative journey to learn to trust your heart as you create with Him. Follow PJ's footsteps through this book and find your place in history!

Theresa Dedmon
Founder of Create Academy
Author, Artist, and Speaker
www.thereasadedmon.com

INTRODUCTION

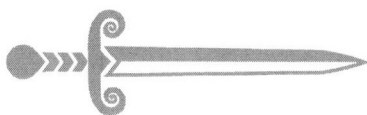

This is a story of how God, the Ultimate Warrior, called out the Warrior in me to face the enemies of fear, tragedy, and loss. It's a story of the fierce struggle of the human spirit to overcome. My desire in sharing my story with you is to shine the light of God on every courageous step you and I take together on this Warrior Dance journey to freedom! You will learn how to activate the Warrior within, step into your true identity, gain control of your life, and identify what you want and why. Through courageous, creative acts, you will be empowered to break free from the shackles holding you back!

The tactics, weapons, and wisdom I share may be surprising, as you will see that my arsenal is full of creativity and the arts.

As we step onto the battlefield of your destiny, we must pass through the darkness before we enter the glory God has for us. But I promise it will be worth it. I want to meet you where you're at on your Warrior Dance journey, and if you choose to go the distance, your transformation will be imminent. My prayer is for you to come through this battle with increased confidence in who you are, your voice, and your expression as a creative.

Let us lock arms as we pass from darkness to glory. Through brave acts of courage, we'll move forward into the glorious promises God has given each one of us.

We stand at the threshold of your Warrior Awakening.

Can you see it? Look closer. There it is. Your destiny's waiting for you!

WARRIOR DANCE:
THE STORY

As I held the flag in my hand, it became like a sword. I felt an anointing as I began waving it and wielding it in the presence of the Lord. At that moment, I was the only one there. I encountered a level of intimacy I had never experienced before. It was as though the Lord was consummating our relationship. That night, all starry-eyed, I could hardly sleep as I savored this extraordinary breakthrough in the spirit. My worship became more intercessory and warlike. I felt the atmosphere shift as I worshiped with all my heart. The movement in my dance not only transformed me, but transported me in a sense, into a heavenly, holy realm where battles would be fought, and victory would be their end.

PART ONE

WARRIOR DEFINED

AND FREEDOM

FROM WHAT?

CHAPTER ONE

ME? A WARRIOR?

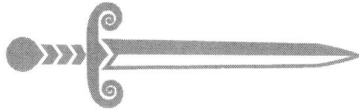

She is a light, a fire, a thunder in the desert
God placed a mission in her through demonstration of His gifts
Although her life was wrought with obstacles and entanglements
And the enemy of her soul pursued her vehemently
Because of the call on her life
She, with the help of The One,
resisted and pushed back the darkness
With arrows, clashing of swords, and fierce battles
She would never give up, nor would she surrender
One day she would see the victory won and stand before her Beloved
A shining star... bold, brave, and beautiful!

Life begins. Sounds of a heartbeat, full of life and wonder. A tiny flicker of a Warrior's heart in the making. Each one is different. We all must find our way. Through the good and bad. Joy and sadness. Laughter and tears. Strengths and weaknesses. Winning or losing.

I believe we all want the good, the joy and laughter, to be strong, and to win in life.

But what about the bad, the sadness and tears, when we're weak and experience loss?

We live in an intricate balance of a Warrior's Dance.

We step onto the battlefield, like David, who danced, leading the procession into victory.

The battle.

The battle is where the Warrior is accessed. The battle is where we fight alongside our Warrior God.

But what makes a Warrior? How does one become a Warrior?

We will see as we pass from darkness to glory.

HEARTBEATS OF LIFE AND WONDER

But you are a chosen people, a royal priesthood, a holy nation, God's special possession, that you may declare the praises of him who called you out of darkness into his wonderful light. 1 Peter 2:9 (NIV)

Darkness…deep darkness. I could push it back for a time and act like everything was all right, but the darkness would return even stronger. I had no idea how to fight against this hell. I couldn't sleep. I was anxious all the time. My thoughts were dark and tormenting. Captive to an unseen foe, I didn't want to fight. I wanted out, to retreat and run, far, far away.

It was the 1960s. My neighborhood brought many a starry night filled with friendships, games, and wonderment. My friends meant everything to me. Like most kids, we played Kick the Can, Hide-and-Seek, Red Rover, and other childhood games. With high adventures on the trampoline, we'd soar through the air seemingly without a care in the world!

But these weren't simply childhood fun and games. Not to me. This was serious business as I showed up with all the courage and bravery I could muster.

I lived for these summer nights.

At a giant park nearby, towering cottonwood trees stood like sentinels, watching guard as we forged our way into this habitat of wilderness and trails that led to imaginary worlds.

We were like trailblazers in a land not yet discovered.

The canal behind our house gave us the opportunity to explore in our search for crawdads, snakes, and frogs. In this naturalist paradise of science and nature, we gathered specimens where we watched tadpoles turn to frogs and found abandoned pincers and snakeskins left behind.

With winter came snowmen, sledding, and snowball fights. When skating, I'd imagine myself carving out figure eights, leaping with perfect precision, and breaking free from my limitations!

At Christmas, our street became a display of old-fashioned holiday spirit. The houses came aglow with warm welcomes, candles, and the smell of baked goods.

I held these memories like a locket inside my heart.

Where does the Warrior come in; you ask?

You will soon see as the brightness and wonder of my youth started to fade into gray, and the courage in my heart began to weaken.

WHAT IS A WARRIOR?

What does it mean to be a Warrior? Who were the Warriors in the Bible? Who were the Warriors in history?

> Merriam-Webster defines a Warrior as "a person engaged or experienced in warfare: a person engaged in some struggle or conflict."[1]

> Webster's Revised Unabridged Dictionary says a Warrior is someone "engaged or experienced in war, or in military life; a soldier; a champion."[2]

WARRIORS IN THE BIBLE

The Bible is filled with Warriors and their exploits.

The first mention of God being a Warrior is Moses's song to the Lord after God rescued them, miraculously making a way across the Red Sea as Pharaoh, his chariots, and the entire army succumbed to a watery grave.

The Lord is a Warrior, the Lord is his name! Exodus 15:3 (NIV)

Isaiah wrote the following explosive words describing God as a Warrior in a "New Song of Praise."

The Lord will march forth like a mighty hero; He will come out like a Warrior, full of fury. He will shout his battle cry and crush all his enemies. Isaiah 42:13 (NLT)

You could hear the prophet Jeremiah's heart cry when everything he believed in was falling apart.

But the Lord is with me as a dread warrior; therefore my persecutors will stumble; they will not overcome me. They will be greatly shamed, for they will not succeed. Their eternal dishonor will never be forgotten. Jeremiah 20:11 (ESV)

King David proclaims the victory we have in God as our Warrior: Through God we will do valiantly, and it is He who will trample down our enemies! Psalm 60:12 (NASB)

I believe we all have a Warrior in us because God is a Warrior.

From the beginning of time in Genesis, with the fall of man, we read about the powerful testimonies of God's people: fighting against the enemy, enduring suffering and captivity, time and again…only to see God's faithfulness to His people rise to every occasion and secure their victory.

Joshua, the mighty man of God, delivers the people of Israel to the Promised Land by God's direction, then later defeats the enemy as he marches around the walls of Jericho, and they fall.

Gideon, the unlikely timid Warrior whom God called his "Mighty Man of Valor," delivers the Israelites from the oppression and heavy hand of the Midianites.

In the New Testament, we see a life like no other—Jesus the Ultimate Warrior. Through His miraculous birth, unjustifiable death, and victorious resurrected life, He compels us to radical change in our beliefs and how we live.

Through His extraordinary acts of love, Jesus conquered death and fulfilled the Law of Moses's two primary commands:

> Love the Lord your God with all your heart and with all your soul and with all your mind and with all your strength. The second is this: "Love your neighbor as yourself." Mark 12:30-31 (NIV)

In the Gospels and the book of Acts, we see ordinary men become Warriors. As eyewitnesses to His Majesty, they saw firsthand the life of Jesus, born in the flesh. Breaking the barrier between God and man, shining His glorious light of grace upon their broken human condition.

We watch with disbelief as the Apostle Peter, Simon by birth, denies Jesus in his greatest time of need. Later he is restored and called by his new name, Peter, Petra ('Rock'), on which Jesus would build his church.

The Apostle John, "whom Jesus loved," is one of the first to believe in the Resurrection and would later write the book of Revelation.

Then the unexpected happened.

The Apostle Paul, known as Saul, a proud, righteous, educated Jew, and ruthless persecutor of Christians, was radically changed after being blinded by the power of the Holy Spirit. This transformation would cause an explosion in Paul that ignited the passion for spreading the Gospel message like wildfire to the Gentile and Roman worlds.

I identify with these courageous Warriors from the Bible.

I am emboldened and strengthened by God's Warrior Heart for us.

These stories have become an arsenal in my life, as armor and weapons to fight against the enemy.

BRAVEHEART

The movie *Braveheart* affected me greatly. Why? I was moved by the urgent cry of William Wallace's heart as demonstrated in his "Freedom Speech":

"Sons of Scotland, I am William Wallace…and I see a whole army of my countrymen, here, in defiance of Tyranny. You've come to fight as free men and free men you are. What will you do without freedom? Will you fight?" [3]

QR Code #1 - Freedom Speech
Braveheart (1995) - Best scene - William Wallace's speech (HD)

William Wallace's strong desire to have a country of his own was birthed when he was a young boy. Seen in the tyranny of the English upon his home and countrymen, who had given in to English rule, even the King of Scotland and his noblemen had submitted to political serfdom in order to keep their comforts and positions.

So, when Wallace meets the heir to the throne, Robert the Bruce, Wallace pleads with him to "unite the clans." Wallace assured Bruce that if he would just lead the people of Scotland and fight, they would follow him to victory.

Like William Wallace, I see an entire army of courageous Warriors in the body of Christ. I believe that you are one of them!

My questions for you are:

- Are you ready to awaken the Warrior within?
- Will you seize this critical time in history, to fight the battles needed to win your freedom? Your destiny?

My Warrior friend, I believe you will rise to the occasion because God placed something extraordinary inside you. And just as He did with me, God desires to awaken the Warrior within so you can fight and win on the battlefields of life!

QUESTIONS:

1. What was your life like growing up?

2. What words and stories speak to the Warrior in your heart?

3. Who are the heroes in your life, and how have you identified with them? Why?

PART TWO

DARK CLOUDS

AND DEEP PITS

CHAPTER TWO

GOD, WHERE ARE YOU?

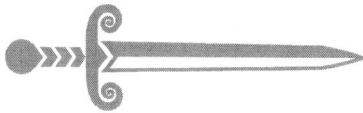

Her conquering knight was with her.
As she ran to face the giant
Who had tormented her soul,
A strange thing happened.
Instead of becoming bigger
As she approached him
He became smaller.
This "big bully" was merely a facade.
She began to see his form take the shape
Of a dark plume of smoke that dissipated
As she gained ground.

My Warrior's heart beats with deep compassion knowing many of you will understand some of these same frailties, sorrows, and tragedies I've passed through.

I believed *Four Warrior Lies* that would later become my demise.

Let us take up our armor of courage as we step into the dark places of my life.

THE BATTLE OF GOOD AND EVIL RAGES ON

God speaks to me through movies. The emotions I feel are strong. I connect on a deep level when I see good win over evil. I sense at that moment, I, too, am victorious, that I can do it and overcome the dark clouds and deep pits of life.

But like Eowyn in *Lord of the Rings: The Two Towers*, I thought I'd never fulfill God's call on my life.

In the story, the kingdom of Rohan is preparing for war. Eowyn, niece of King Theoden, has the heart of a Warrior. While brandishing her sword, she turns and finds herself face to face with Aragorn as their two swords clash.

> Aragorn - "You have some skill with a blade."
> Eowyn - "The women of this country long ago learned that those without swords could soon die upon them. I fear neither death nor pain."
> Aragorn - "What do you fear my lady?"
> Eowyn - "A cage. To stay behind bars until use and old age accept them and all chance of valor has gone beyond recall or desire."
> Aragorn – "You're a daughter of kings. A shieldmaiden of Rohan. I do not think that will be your fate."[4]

QR Code #2: Eowyn and Aragorn
Lord of the Rings: The Two Towers. Eowyn and Aragorn

Eowyn's fear of being metaphorically caged behind bars "until use and old age accept [her hands] and all valor is gone," greatly troubled me.

What would be my fate? Would I fight, or would I retreat when all valor is gone?

MY FAMILY

Church was important to me. God was strong. I needed Him. My heart took courage when I stood with my family, and together, we sang old hymns expressing humanity's heart cry. The beauty of these songs, our voices united, speaking forth what we believe...these words of faith were imprinted on my soul and woven into every fiber of my being. There was love there, a wonderment surrounding the stories, seasons, and celebrations.

My family roots go deep in the Nebraska farmlands. Family reunions at the family farm brought lively discussions and talks of the good ol' days. On display were old black-and-white photographs of my dad's staunch German relatives who had migrated from Germany in the late 1800s.

Farming was hard work. Faith was important to them.

Those hearty generations witnessed the epic historical events of World War I, the Great Depression, the Dust Bowl, and World War II.

My mom's family goes as far back as the Mayflower and the American Revolution. They passed down stories of the pioneer days journeying across the country in covered wagons.

This family legacy embodied resilience. Strength was there.

Together, my parents' strong faith, love of nature, music, and the arts would be woven into our lives as they raised their family of four and navigated through life's challenges.

My brother was the oldest, followed by my two sisters and me.

I fondly think of a composite picture of the four of us in birth order, all at about the age of three, hanging in my parent's home.

My brother was a beautiful little boy with light brown hair combed neatly to the side and big hazel eyes full of curiosity.

But something wasn't right. My brother's development was slow. He didn't progress like the other children. At the age of twelve, my brother was diagnosed with mild retardation and epilepsy.

The first memory of my brother having a seizure was when I was four. My sisters and I were rushed to the neighbor's house after he had fallen and cracked his head open.

This would be the first of many.

The forcefulness of these seizures caused my brother to fall hard to the ground with involuntary convulsions and violent jerking movements, lasting several minutes.

These seizures frightened me. I was scared, terrified really. I felt powerless and would often run and hide behind the door until it was all over.

I'd see people staring, pointing, and even laughing at my brother, in public. I wanted to stand up and defend him, yet something inside pulled me back down. I didn't say anything because I believed nice Christian girls didn't do that. But deep within my heart, I felt angry. How could people be so insensitive, hurtful, and unkind?

My sisters were three and four years older than me. Our identities growing up were the oldest being the "artist and comedian" and my middle sister being the "musician and reliable one." She and I shared a room. I relied on her a lot because my mom had so much to deal with. She was there for me and wasn't afraid to stand up to the bullies in my life. When I felt fearful and didn't know what to do, I would run to her where I felt safe.

MY SCHOOL YEARS

The best part about school was being in gym class or on the playground. I'd race with my friends, do flips on the bars, and play tirelessly at tetherball or volleyball. Field Day was like the Olympics to me. I felt proud of my blue ribbons in the high jump, broad jump, and relay races. I wanted to be tough like the Warrior I felt inside.

WARRIOR LIE №1 YOUR WORTH IS BASED ON PERFORMANCE, LOOKS, AND POPULARITY

Then one day, a new girl showed up. She beat me in everything. All those blue ribbons turned to red. She followed me into junior high and high school. When trying out for cheerleader, she was chosen, not me.

My plans to be in the talent show didn't work out either. Whether in choir, art class, or theater, I wasn't picked for the part, applauded, or celebrated. I felt like I didn't matter and wasn't good enough. In my mind, I felt defeated and like a failure.

I didn't feel or look much like a Warrior either. By junior high, I was the epitome of a teeny bopper; awkward, tall, and gangly, with braces and pimples. I embarrassed easily. Now I was terrified of being noticed or called on in class. I felt more comfortable being a number, a nobody, to blend in. My outgoing, fun personality started to fade away.

My Warrior Heart began to beat with less passion and courage.

By the time I entered high school, my faith waned; I wanted to give my heart entirely to God. But over time, I found when I went to apply my faith, it was difficult, lonely, and quite frankly, no fun at all.

I could relate to Gideon, who was from the weakest clan and least of his father's house. The Angel of the Lord appeared to him under the terebinth tree and said:

"The Lord is with you, mighty warrior!"

"Pardon me, my lord," Gideon replied, "but if the LORD is with us, why has all this happened to us?" Judges 6:12-13a (NIV)

Like Gideon, I asked, "Why did all this happen to me?"

I had given up and hid under the tree, with little hope of making a difference. Where was my Warrior Heart now?

I was mad at God. Why was being a Christian so hard? Where was the joy and strength I once felt? I wanted to have fun, to be wild and free. My awkwardness turned to teenage beauty. I was being noticed. It felt good to hang out with the

WARRIOR LIE № 2
REBELLION IS POWER.

rebels. Weekends were for carousing, parties, and the bar scene. It seemed to take away the loneliness and pain of being shy, insecure, and average.

The strong influence of a significant moral shift in the culture compounded things. It was a time of great conflict and change. There I was right in the middle of it all with rock and roll, hippies and drugs, the fallout and protests of the Vietnam War, the Jesus Movement, Women's "Liberation," Roe vs. Wade, and the legalization of abortion.

I was riding the wave of rebellion and headed for a massive crash.

GOD'S PROTECTION

Tragedy struck only a few weeks after graduation. I knew something was wrong that morning. After my boyfriend came to pick me up, he was driving recklessly, passing on the median, speeding, going too fast up windy mountain roads. I knew this was not good. I slid down in the seat. I faintly spoke up and said to stop, but not loud enough. He kept going. I felt unsafe and didn't know what to do...more mountain turns. We were headed to a camp he used to work at...turn after winding turn, on it went, and then suddenly, on the next turn, the small open convertible flipped and was on top of us. We hit the pavement hard, skidding across the road with great force, sending shock waves through my body, when suddenly, the car came to a halt.

I reached for my boyfriend but felt and heard nothing. Covered by darkness and a chilling silence. I waited encased and trapped for the wreckage to be lifted off us. Next, I remember someone helping me to the side of the road. My first thought was, where's my boyfriend?

I was taken by ambulance to a nearby hospital. Shortly after arriving, I passed out.

The impact from the pavement resulted in deep skin abrasions on my right arm, wrist, and cheekbone. It was a miracle I had no internal injuries; however, this tragic moment in time would cause repercussions of emotional pain for years to come.

WARRIOR LIE № 3
PUSH THE PAIN
AWAY.

Somewhere in the blur of all this, I found out my boyfriend had been killed instantly. I was able to hold it together at the funeral as I thought to myself, "It wasn't my fault, I told him to stop, but he just kept going."

Without any intervention or counseling, I returned to how I was living before.

In the meantime, God in His mercy waited and waited, until I was ready. Through rebellion, death, sin, and my pride, He waited, ever so patiently.

But the time was not yet...

In the movie *The Last of the Mohicans*,[5] set during the French and Indian War, there's a famous scene where Nathaniel, a colonist who was adopted by the Mohican tribe, has fallen in love with Cora, the daughter of a British Colonel. Both are caught in a military conflict between the British and the English.

WARRIOR LIE №4 DON'T FACE THE ENEMY OF FEAR.

In the scene, "I Will Find You," Nathaniel makes the courageous choice to separate from Cora in hopes that he will have a better chance of fighting against the murderous pursuit of the French scout, Magua.

QR Code #3: Mohicans
The Last of the Mohicans (2/5) Movie CLIP - I Will Find You! (1992) HD

Would my Warrior God pursue me like that? Even in my rebellion, pride, and sin?

DEEP SADNESS

Two years later, another tragedy struck our family.

My parents did the best they could with my brother. When he became working age, he was admitted into a group home for adult men. There he could work at a factory and live on his own. His house parents were a loving married couple; however, the single man that worked weekends butted heads with my brother. One weekend, the man got angry at my brother, beat him, and pushed him down the stairs. This violent assault put my brother in the hospital with kidney failure. After being discharged, he stayed at my parent's home while he continued to recover. A few days later, he went into cardiac arrest. My older sister, who watched over him while my parents and my other sister were outside, alerted them that something was wrong. My middle sister, who knew CPR, tried to resuscitate him, but to no avail, and he died at the young age of twenty-five.

The courts only gave the offender a *slap on the hand* and told him he couldn't work at adult homes anymore.

My middle sister told me of a time after my brother died when my parents went fishing. My dad just let the boat go round and round in the middle of the lake where they both cried over the loss of their son.

My mom was never the same after that. Later, at the young age of sixty, she had an early onset of dementia. I attribute this to the great grief and sorrow she felt after losing her son.

I never heard my parents' express bitterness or anger, or condemn the man who did this. Through this, they imparted an amazing testimony of love and forgiveness to us.

I began to grow weary of the sadness and shallowness of my life.

Was this the kind of life I wanted? It was time for a change.

The foundation of God's love and truth was about to be restored.

QUESTIONS:

1. What happens when you fail? When you fall? When tragedy strikes?

2. What are some of the lies you believe about yourself?

3. How can you overcome and learn from your mistakes?

THE FOUR WARRIOR LIES I BELIEVED:

Warrior Lie #1: Your worth is based on performance, looks, and popularity.

Warrior Lie #2: Rebellion is power.

Warrior Lie #3: Push the pain away.

Warrior Lie #4: Don't face the enemy of fear.

CHAPTER THREE

DISCOVERING GOD

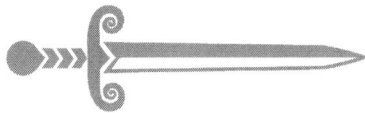

"Show me Heaven," she asked.
"Show me the place where You dwell.
Open my eyes to Your world of love, grace, and joy."
As her eyes stayed on Him,
She could see, however small,
Blue sky and clouds of gold and splendor.
She could see the river of life flowing…
Teaming with fresh, sparkling clean, pure water
That was so alive.

Warrior, it's time to rise up and face the darkness with determination and courage!

Watch as I discover God, my Valiant Warrior, shine His glorious light that brings "blue sky, gold, and splendor" to the dark places of my soul.

I identified nine Warrior weapons that helped me to overcome.

Disclaimer: The decisions I made regarding my battle with depression are from my experience. If you struggle in these ways, please know I am not giving any medical advice and am in no way telling you how to choose a certain way. This is what worked for me and is part of my story. I found these "weapons" helped me on the road to health and healing.

ADULT YEARS, MARRIAGE, AND CHILDREN

I met my husband in college, a 6'8" basketball player—tall, dark, and handsome. It didn't take long to discover we were very much in love and were married two years later.

He would be the man I would later call my "earthly rock."

I began to return to God and started reading the Bible. I wanted to change. I was searching. Impacted by the book by Hannah Whitall Smith called, *The Christian's Secret of a Happy Life*, I was growing spiritually. My heart was soft toward the Lord again. I felt my Warrior Heart stirring in me.

Additionally, I was greatly influenced by a popular movie at the time called, *Norma Rae*. The courage I felt inside my heart could identify with this woman's courage to speak out for crucial change when confronted with great sadness and injustice in her life.

Norma Rae[6] is a true story about a single mother who works at the local textile factory along with her parents. One day, a labor activist arrives in town because of the poor working conditions and corrupt management. He soon finds his ally in Norm Rae. Spurred on by her father's untimely death from heat and exhaustion, she joins in the fight for change to confront the management and persuade her coworkers to unionize. After being fired for not complying with their demands, she takes a piece of cardboard and writes "Union" on it, then jumps up on her worktable, holding the sign up high. Slowly turning for all to see, they begin to shut off their machines, one by one. Eventually, the mill becomes silent. This spontaneous act of courage moves in the hearts of her coworkers, bringing the votes needed.

QR Code #4: Norma Rae
Norma Rae, Martin Ritt, 1979 - Union Sign Scene

I share this scene because I believe ALL Warriors have a Norma Rae moment in them. Norma had found her voice, and I needed to find mine.

The reality of this new life with my husband's family, friends, and family business began to affect me. A sad reminder of my past overshadowed my short happy beginning. It seemed every insecurity, weakness, and awkward part of me resurfaced.

All that I had mustered up to cope and survive in life, and the fun, carefree image I had tried to portray, no longer worked. Though I had turned back to God, I struggled. Where was He? Why wasn't He helping me through this? I felt lonely. I was drowning in memories of insecurity, defeat, and the pain I had tried to cover up.

THE UNWELCOME VISITOR OF DEPRESSION

These insecurities caused me to draw closer to God in hopes I would feel better. But in my mind, negative emotions began to enter my thoughts.

My mind soon became a fierce battleground. Strong emotions of anger and self-hatred began to wear down my defenses. I could push them back for a time and act like everything was all right, but the darkness would return even stronger. I had no idea how to fight against this hell. I couldn't sleep. I was anxious all the time. My thoughts were dark and tormenting, captive to an unseen foe. I didn't want to fight. I wanted out, to retreat, run far, far away and hide.

There was no Warrior in sight.

The fog of loneliness and sadness gave way to a long season of depression.

After trying all sorts of natural remedies, I turned to tranquilizers, thinking maybe with a bit of help from medication, it would just go away. When that didn't bring any change, I became even more despondent.

My husband was having a hard time, too. He had only known the fun, party, carefree side of me. When he was unable to help, I'd get so furious. I was like a caged prisoner, with anger and even outbursts of rage. My sobbing turned into deep, guttural groanings. I didn't understand what was wrong with me.

The suffering and pain became unbearable.

I needed help.

I made an appointment with a counselor. I began to describe the fierce battle in my mind and the dark tormenting thoughts I experienced. This began the grueling process of me talking about my past. Months and months went by.

After a year of talking, it out, it was time for our daughter to be born. Having her brought new hope into my life. My sleep and peace returned. I felt I had a purpose and began to engage in life again.

My depression seemed to be gone, but as you will soon see, the battle was far from over.

THE UNWANTED VISITOR RETURNS

During the next five years, our two sons were born.

Shortly after our youngest son came into our world, I began to feel overwhelmed again. The unwanted visitor of depression returned. I now had the responsibility of caring for three young children. I panicked. I knew how horrible depression could be and how each day feels like you're going through a thick, dark forest with briars and thorns that seem to never end.

Though I lived on a beautiful mountain property surrounded by hiking paths, pine trees, and the smell of beautiful wildflowers, I found my walks no longer refreshed me. My heart was heavy, my spirit weighed down. The colors became gray. I didn't notice the beauty anymore. The sadness and uncertainty of who I was enveloped me.

Once again, I was desperate, dying inside, engulfed in sadness, tormented by the hell inside. I felt so unstable like I could go crazy, going without sleep for days.

I tried to find ways to lift my spirit using positive affirmations, but they were just words to me. I read book after book on self-help, self-esteem, and self-love. None of them could reach this deep, dark place in me. At times in utter frustration, I'd throw them against the wall.

WARRIOR, RISE UP AND FACE THE DARKNESS

But I was determined to find the answer. I got a large medical book at the library and looked up the diagnosis for depression, mental illness, obsessive-compulsive, and other disorders. Many descriptions fit my symptoms of insomnia, anxiety, obsessive thoughts, and mood swings. It could be any one of these things.

WARRIOR WEAPON №1 ASK–SEEK–KNOCK

The prognosis they depicted painted a bleak future. Was this what God wanted for me? I couldn't accept this as my plight. God's Word spoke of freedom, victory, and deliverance.

That's when the Warrior rose up in me as I slammed the book closed, shoved it aside, and said, "NO!" I didn't have the answers, but that would not be me!

WARRIOR WEAPON №2 THE POWER OF "NO"

I was now ready to fight.

The answers started coming. While reading a book by Corrie ten Boom, *Amazing Love: True Stories of the Power of Forgiveness*, my eyes came to an abrupt halt as I read the following text:

WARRIOR WEAPON №3 HOPE

> "Jesus Christ is able to untangle all the snarls in your soul, to banish ALL your complexes, and to transform even your fixed habit patterns, no matter how deeply they are etched in your subconscious."[7]

Untangle ALL the snarls in my soul?

Banish ALL my complexes?

No matter how DEEPLY they were etched in my subconscious?

These words of unquestionable faith endued huge breaths of courageous hope into me. I could certainly embrace these ideas if this woman who survived the Holocaust believed them.

WARRIOR WEAPON №4 COURAGE

Next, the miracle in the bathroom brought more breakthrough.

As I cried out to God on my knees, I opened my Bible. The pages fell open to Romans 7.

> I have discovered this principle of life—that when I want to do what is right, I inevitably do what is wrong. I love God's law with all my heart. But there is another power within me that is at war with my mind. This power makes me a slave to the sin that is still within me. Oh, what a miserable person I am! Who will free me from this life that is dominated by sin and death? Thank God! The answer is in Jesus Christ our Lord... Romans 7:21-25a (NLT)

As I read these words, they began to clearly reveal my crippled spiritual condition.

I wanted to do what was right but so often came up short.

There was a war going on in my mind.

I wasn't free, and I knew it. The power of sin had enslaved me.

I was indeed miserable. I wanted freedom from the grip sin had on my life.

God was gloriously shining the light of His Word into the dark crevices of my soul!

WARRIOR WEAPON №5 THE POWER OF FORGIVENESS

As God began to expose the dark crevices, He began to convict me of a specific sin. My rebellion and wild living had opened doors to immoral thinking. The issue of abortion needed to be faced head-on. As I sat there alone, watching the movie *Silent Scream*[8] at a local church, I saw the graphic, raw truth about abortion. The stark realization of ending the life of an unborn child filled me with immense regret, guilt, and shame. Although I had not had an abortion, I had supported those who did. As I drove home that night, with tears streaming down my face, I cried out to God, and in that dire moment, I knew He had forgiven me. The power of forgiveness coursed through me like a cleansing fire, turning me 180 degrees, never to believe that lie again.

Jesus had reached into the deep, dark places of my heart with His glorious truth and set me free!

> God's law was given so that all people could see how sinful they were. But as people sinned more and more, God's wonderful grace became more abundant. Romans 5:20 (NLT)

Next came a voice of truth on the radio. The topic was spiritual warfare and the dark forces that can attack the mind. I was shocked. I had never heard anyone talk about this before.

WARRIOR WEAPON №6 IDENTITY IN CHRIST

After meeting with the counselor whose voice of truth I had heard on the radio, he strongly advised me to read the book, *Handbook to Happiness*,[9] by Dr. Charles R. Solomon.

The words came like a mighty rushing river into my dry and thirsty soul as I read them.

I had been in a drought, and the rain was beginning to fall! The answers kept coming.

The following verse released a thunderous revelation of what Christ's death and resurrection life fully accomplished for me on the cross:

WARRIOR WEAPON №7 TRANSFORMATION

> I have been crucified with Christ and I no longer live, but Christ lives in me. The life I now live in the body, I live by faith in the Son of God, who loved me and gave himself for me. Galatians. 2:20 (NIV)

As I turned the pages again, I was completely awe-struck by a diagram called *The Wheel and the Line*,[10] divinely designed by the author. It was the concept of Galatians 2:20 in picture form.

This visual was vital to my understanding, opening my eyes wide to the truth of my identification with Christ's death and resurrection.

This is what Dr. Solomon called *The Exchanged Life*.

QR CODE #5: Wheel & Line
Wheel & Line – A Guide to Freedom Through the Cross

QR CODE #6: I Am In Christ
I Am In Christ

WARRIOR WEAPON №8 DON'T GIVE UP– KEEP GOING

God gave me a friend as I began to step into my new identity. With a lawyer background, her logical mind helped my unstable reasoning mind. I needed spiritual toughness. Firm black and white lines with no obscurity. She would say to me, "PJ, either you believe it (God's Word), or you don't." And on bad days, she reminded me, "Get up and brush your teeth." In other words, don't give up; keep going!

These simple phrases became a Godly yoke to guide me on hard days.

The difficult process of untangling my mind didn't happen overnight. The unhealthy patterns didn't want to go. Over and over my emotions would try to pull me back down to all the broken pieces of my soul. The learning process was gut-wrenching, but I kept on, knowing I would get better.

I was beginning to train my mind, will, and emotions, like a true Warrior, on how to live in a totally different way.

My emotional world had been backward. I had relied on people and things to make me happy. Being led by my feelings made me very unstable emotionally and spiritually. My shaky faith then led me into frustration, anger, and defeat. But when I put God's Word first, faith would follow, resulting in my feelings coming into alignment with the truth.

WARRIOR WEAPON №9 FACT–FAITH– FEELING

In other words, I would choose to believe God's Word, apply it by faith, and trust it to be true. My feelings would then follow and line up, like a trained soldier—*fact, faith, feelings*. This new way of thinking would soon bring the stability I so desperately needed.

The Warrior in me was being trained and awakened!

With these nine Warrior Weapons at the core, you will grow stronger for the journey ahead and be well on your way to victorious living. Onward!

QUESTIONS:

1. Have you ever "turned your face to the wall" and said "no" like I did to receive your healing? (Read about Hezekiah in Isaiah 38:2)

2. How have you overcome and found true freedom?

3. What Warrior Weapons are in your arsenal? Which weapons could you add?

Warriors need the Word of God as their sword on the battlefield. As we review the Nine Warrior Weapons, be sure to take note of the corresponding scripture verse applied to each one.

Warrior Weapon #1: Ask - Seek - Knock
> Warrior, be determined to find an answer and trust God to show you the way!
> Jeremiah 29:13

Warrior Weapon #2: The Power of "No"
> Warrior, rise up and say "No" to your flesh, the world, and the enemy's lies. Watch fear go, and your faith grow!
> 1 John 4:18

Warrior Weapon #3: Hope
> Trust God to impart hope to you through His Word and the words of other Warriors.
> Romans 4:18

Warrior Weapon #4: Courage
> Warrior, take steps of courage that'll lead you to the answers that will set you free!
> Joshua 1:9

Warrior Weapon #5: The Power of Forgiveness
> Renewal begins with true repentance. Turn from your sin, repent and receive total forgiveness!
> Acts 3:19

Warrior Weapon #6: Identity in Christ
> Warrior, contend for your identity in Christ with God's Word as your sword!
> Hebrews 4:12

Warrior Weapon #7: Transformation
> Walk out *The Exchanged Life* daily and be strengthened by other Warriors in the process.
> Galatians 2:20

Warrior Weapon #8: Don't Give Up - Keep Going!
> This new way of living takes some hard work, so don't give up, Warrior. Keep going!
> Galatians 6:9

Warrior Weapon #9: Fact - Faith - Feelings
> Become like a trained soldier and let Fact - Faith - Feelings lead the way to freedom!
> Philippians 4:6-8

DISCOVERING YOUR

VOICE THROUGH

THE ARTS

CHAPTER FOUR

WARRIOR TACTICS FOR

THE BATTLEFIELD

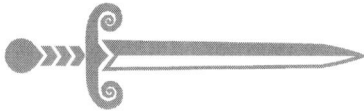

The voice of freedom
Started to rise up within her
Stronger and stronger
With every praise
Her steps were strengthened.
The cry of her heart
Would soon be answered
All that she had held inside
And tried to untangle
Was now given a voice
A place of expression
To praise, to dance
To find joy again
The music within her heart
Began to take flight and sing!

I have found my voice. I will not be silenced anymore. My voice matters! My voice makes a difference! When I'm writing. When I'm painting. When I'm dancing. When I'm praying. [i]

There is joy in my voice!

My voice is becoming louder.

With creative *dunamis* power from heaven, I express God's glory with my voice!

THE WORLD NEEDS YOUR VOICE!

At the beginning of the movie *Wonder Woman*,[12] we see a fearless little girl full of confidence, bravery, and courage. Her name is Princess Diana. Her mother, the Queen of the Amazons, and all the women Warriors live on a mythical island called Themyscira. Princess Diana has a virtuous heart with a strong will to fight evil and bring justice. Unbeknownst to her, she was born with superhero powers. Her mission: to be the *god-killer* who will destroy Ares, the evil god of war!

QR Code #7: Wonder Woman
Young Diana : Wonder Woman

We're called to be God's superheroes, like Princess Diana. Through our art, we are a voice that brings justice to a broken and hurting world.

HOW TO SURVIVE THE GREAT
SADNESSES OF LIFE

We're faced with a choice when we find ourselves in a place of great sadness or difficulty. We can choose to resist and prolong the process, or we can take up our Warrior Weapon of courage.

When I could no longer ignore the intense emotions of depression, I got help.

In my search for healing, I discovered the nine Warrior Weapons that brought the truth I needed to set me free. I was now ready for God to show me four unconventional weapons of warfare through the arts that led to a more remarkable victory on the battlefield.

My discovery: *Four Warrior Tactics and Decrees of Courage*. FORWARD!

Tactic: "An action or strategy, carefully planned to achieve a specific end."[13]

Decree: "An official order issued by a legal authority."[14]

WARRIOR TACTIC №1: JOURNALING - BE A WORLD-CHANGER

"If you want to change the world, pick up a pen and write!"[15]
Martin Luther

My world had been turned upside down. The freedom I encountered with the Lord and my newfound identity caused me to search even deeper into my relationship with Him.

In my pursuit, I discovered a life-changing tactic in the book ***Writing to the Father***,[16] by Jackie Jacobsen. This small-but-mighty booklet opened my eyes to the transformative power of writing directly to God and, in turn, hearing His voice.

Journaling revolutionized my life. I recovered my voice. God's divine creative ability began to flow onto the pages. Journaling opened the floodgates to a vibrant, living, loving, intimate exchange with my Heavenly Father.

Maybe you've tried journaling with minimal results. I want to challenge you to look at journaling through fresh eyes. See from a Warrior's perspective as you pick up your pen and write with intention and purpose.

Begin with God's Word. Write any relevant verses, pertinent thoughts, and prayers from your heart. Be earnest and passionate. As you transition, listen for the still small voice of the Holy Spirit. In this place, God's presence becomes strong. These encounters are holy ground as God speaks to you from the throne room of Heaven.

I've considered my collection of journals over these last thirty years to be like Monet's. Each one paints a picture of my life through words. They are a documentary of persevering, overcoming, and staying steadfast with God and His faithfulness to me.

The following excerpt is from one of my journals dated May 18, 2007:

Father God, I ask for Your plan. I listen for Your voice.
My daughter, you are on an unconventional path.
It takes a leader with courage to go down this path —
This path is not "the way"; it is "a way."
I will get you to where you need to be.
I speak increase to your faith.
I speak comfort to your turmoil.
I speak love to your fears.
I will never give up on you. No, never!

Decree: Today, I speak to the world-changer in you to write with new vision, purpose, and passion as you set your feet on the Warrior Path of courage that brings Kingdom change!

QR Code #8: Desert Thunder Arts Website Desert Thunder Arts

Book - The Art and Soul of Journaling - Seven Steps to Greater Intimacy with God

QR Code #9: The Art and Soul of Journaling - YouTube

QR Code #10: Journaling MCPL The Art and Soul of Journaling w/ PJ

WARRIOR TACTIC №2: DANCE AND WORSHIP - ARISE, OH WARRIOR!

Wield your worship weapons. Wield your sword! The time is now: Arise, oh Warrior!

I discovered a love for Israel and grew in my knowledge of Messianic Jewish believers while listening to Sid Roth, *It's Supernatural.* At the end of his program, Paul Wilbur, songwriter and worship leader, would sing the Aaronic Blessing found in Numbers 6:24-26. My heart was captured with a love for worship and giving my all to the Lord Jesus Christ through Messianic dance and praise. Demonstrated so beautifully in Paul Wilbur's video, *Jerusalem Arise!*[17]

Dance has brought a new dimension into my life. It is at the core of my worship where I connect and communicate with God and enter Heaven's atmosphere. Dance can be tender and intimate, deepening my relationship with God, or a place I can fight my battles and express myself with the heart of a Warrior.

When I first discovered worship and dance, it released a divine connection in me. My Warrior Spirit came alive. Like the imagery in Ezekiel 37:1-10, the dry bones described my time of depression—dry, lifeless, with little hope. Then, God's Word began to put muscle and sinew on them as His Holy Spirit breathed into me. My spirit stood up as I came alive through dance. My heart soared with joy in a way I'd never known before.

Whenever I step into this new realm, a "spirit of heaviness" is broken and is replaced with "a garment of praise." (Isaiah 61:3)

Whether worshiping in a group or by myself, I watch the atmosphere change into a joyful, reverent heavenly realm full of God's presence and promises. Here, we grow as Worship Warriors and receive the revelation, healing, and deliverance we so desire.

Journal Entry:

You are a Mighty Warrior
Leading the procession in the desert
I have given you the victory
Over all these things and more!
Take action on this gift I have given you
It's what you were born for!
Lead on, My daughter
Dance over the desert of your soul
To the places I show you
Prepare the way of the Lord
The time has come for you to do this
Rise up, raise the battle cry
Praise and worship Me
In doing so, you will triumph over your enemies!

Decree: I speak to your dance, Worship Warrior. May the breath of God come and breathe new life into your steps, and your movement, as you worship before the Lord!

QR Code #11: Praise Worship Glory

QR Code: #12 Jerusalem Arise - Paul Wilbur

WARRIOR TACTIC №3: CREATING POWERFUL PROPHETIC IMAGES WITH ART

"The essence of creating prophetic art is learning to listen with
the ears of your spirit via your imagination in order to release the
Light and Life of God through the work you create."[18]
Matt Tommey Mentoring

Prophetic art has changed my life. These images have given me powerful breakthroughs of healing, hope, and strength as I enter into unseen worlds from the Kingdom of God.

One of my first drawings was birthed while listening to the song, *Royalty*,[19] by Alberto and Kimberly Rivera. The words, "What do you decree, what do you want to see?" inspired me to draw an image of my true identity in Christ.

Like Queen Esther, I felt the Lord extend His scepter and ask me the same question. There I was, lost in worship as the God of Heaven and all creation asked me, "What do you desire, PJ? Up to half the Kingdom."

I discovered that as I pick up my pencil to draw or my brush to paint, they become a sword in the spiritual realm as I allow the Holy Spirit to wield what's in my heart through drawing and painting. In this creative heavenly atmosphere, God's Word comes alive with breath and spirit as these images take root in my soul to strengthen, guide, and ground me.

As described in the following journal entry:

Lord, show me
How to consistently walk with You
How I am seated with You in heavenly places.

My Daughter,
I see you stately and strong
An oak of righteousness
You are a daughter of kings!
You have found favor in My sight
I give you the Kingdom
Not just half but all of it
You walk in My authority and rulership
Because you are royalty
Continue to soak in My presence
Prepare yourself for what is true intimacy
In this, you will really know who you are
Whatever you request, I will grant it to you.

Decree: I speak to the artist in you to practice expressing your art as a prophetic visual that brings breakthroughs, changes atmospheres, and sets your feet on the Warrior Path to victory!

QR CODE #13: Prophetic Artwork CH 4

WARRIOR TACTIC №4: PASSIONATE PRAYERS - SET ON VICTORY

"…his word is in my heart like a fire, a fire shut up in my bones…"
Jeremiah 20:9 (NIV)

God's Word gives us the foundation and framework to build powerful prayers full of passion and truth. The Psalms show that King David moves from a position of fear to one of faith, from anxiety to peace, and from sadness to hope. Prayers written with rawness and fierceness help us to stand firm in the face of opposition.

These Warrior Prayers become a dynamo of God's Word that explodes with hope, healing, and victory. Like King David, we stand in a position of authority as God's Word enables us to see the desired end from the beginning in our lives. Whether I pick up my pen or speak with my voice, I can shatter words of fear and defeat with God's Word, set on victory.

Journal Entry:

> Lord, my heart is hurting inside.
> I feel so scattered and pulled in so many directions.
> I feel angry and frustrated.
> I don't know what to do about it.
> I want to escape, and there is nowhere to go…
> But You are my resting place,
> My high tower,
> My companion and friend.
> I sense You in the beautiful music I listen to.
> Your heart is a fire within me.
>
> What say You, Lord?
> I Am the music and fire within you
> I Am the passion bottled up inside you
> I Am the Master Artist that expresses my heart through you!

Decree: I speak to your prayers, Warrior, that they will be full of power and the anointing of the Holy Spirit, forged by fire that will shatter the rocks in your life!

Now it's time, Warrior, to focus on your own creative voice and decrees of courage. Charge!

QUESTIONS:

1. What Warrior Tactics can you identify with? Is yours different?

2. What has been your understanding and experience of journaling, art, dance, and prayer? Do you see the important significance they hold?

3. What makes you come alive? Do you have dry bones that need the breath and spirit of God?

A Recap—Four Warrior tactics that bring victory on the battlefield:

Warrior Tactic #1: Journaling - Become a World-Changer
> Write with new vision, purpose, and passion that brings Kingdom change!

Warrior Tactic #2: Dance and Worship – Arise, O Warrior!
> Your steps have the breath of God in your movement and worship before the Lord!

Warrior Tactic #3: Draw and Paint - Powerful Prophetic Images
> Your art brings breakthroughs and changes atmospheres!

Warrior Tactic #4: Passionate Prayers - Set on Victory!
> Your prayers have the power and anointing of the Holy Spirit!

CHAPTER FIVE

ESSENTIAL TOOLS FOR SURVIVAL AND VIBRANT LIVING

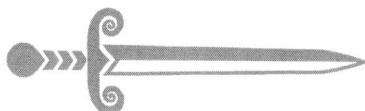

I will wait. I will watch. I will trust.
Walking moment by moment
I walk...
This step, then the next, and the next
She was learning to walk all over again
This step; Rely on Me
This step; Take My hand
This step; Trust
This step; Believe
This step: I've got you
This step: I will lead you
This step; To a life of abundance...

All Warriors need a break from the battle to recover and grow stronger. In the movie *Amazing Grace*, William Wilberforce, a British politician and Independent Member of Parliament, has a conversion while serving. His relationship with John Newton, a former captain of slave ships who turned abolitionist, significantly impacted Wilberforce's leading the movement to abolish the slave trade.

In a memorable scene, Wilberforce plans to pursue influential upper-class voters with a powerful visual, appeasing their senses as they enjoy their tea and crumpets in luxury on a boat. As they pass by *The Madagascar*, Wilberforce, who's standing on the slave trade ship, implores them with these words:

> "Ladies and Gentlemen, this is a slave ship, *The Madagascar*; it has just returned from the Indies, where it delivered 200 men, women, and children to Jamaica. When it left Africa, there were 600 on board; the rest died of disease or despair. That smell is the smell of death. Slow, painful death. Breathe it in. Breathe it deeply. Take those handkerchiefs away from your noses. There now, remember that smell. Remember, *The Madagascar*. Remember that God made men equal."[20]

QR Code #14 - Amazing Grace
Amazing Grace The Madagascar

This brave act of courage, which no amount of words could describe, opened peoples' eyes to the horrific reality of the barbaric slave practices—the result: an unforgettable change of heart.

William Wilberforce needed powerful creative ways to reach people of apathy.

This persuasive visual helped bring the victory he needed to complete the call on his life.

Brave acts of courage are one of the essential tools we need as Warriors.

ESSENTIAL TOOLS FOR SURVIVAL

My freedom from depression required essential tools as I trained my mind to turn from destructive patterns and crippling wrong thinking. The following short phrases were given to me by significant people in my life. These edicts gave me laser focus, placing my feet back on the road to freedom.

I believe God anointed these words and phrases.

CHOOSE TO GET WELL

"When Jesus saw him lying there and learned that he had been in this condition for a long time, he asked him, 'Do you want to get well?'"
John 5:6 (NIV)

Time and time again, I would cry out to God. Like the lame man on the mat, I would lay there paralyzed, not knowing what to do. Depression enveloped me. Anxiety held me in its grip. Fear put me behind bars, making me feel there was no way out. But the misery I felt and the choices before me caused me to search with all my heart for the answers and truth I needed. The options were to surrender to a life of depression, anxiety, and fear, or choose the hard path, face my fears, and find true freedom.

The Warrior Heart in me had a strong desire for freedom, prodding me to make a choice to get well, get up, and receive my healing.

- Search with all your heart.
- Make a choice to get well.
- Receive your healing.

Warrior, I see strength in you to stand, pick up your mat, and walk fully in your healing!

GET UP AND BRUSH YOUR TEETH

"Jesus told him, 'Stand up, pick up your mat, and walk!'"
John 5:8 (NLT)

This simple phrase, "Get up and brush your teeth," coined by a friend, kept my mind from going down the rabbit hole of unending, tortured reasoning. Prompting me to ask myself, no matter how I felt, sleep or no sleep, happy or not happy, hopeful or not hopeful, I needed to choose to get up and brush my teeth! This phrase rallied me to not give in to my flesh and have a pity party over my condition or circumstances. Whatever was going on was only temporary, and it would pass. Life was not going to be this way forever. So, I had a choice. Would I give in and lay there another thirty-eight years and do nothing, or would I rally the Warrior in me to get up, brush my teeth, and get going?

As I encouraged myself, you can do the same through the following actions:

- Rally your spirit.
- Choose to get up and brush your teeth.
- Know that "This, too, shall pass!"

Warrior, together, we can keep from going down the rabbit hole, knowing this, too, shall pass!

FACT - FAITH - FEELING

"Though an army besiege me, my heart will not fear;
though war break out against me, even then I will be confident."
Psalm 27:3 (NIV)

The Word of God was the truth my mind needed. As I applied it by faith, my feelings and emotions would then line up like a soldier in boot camp.

Figuratively, I arrived untrained, out of shape. Over time, the discipline of daily exercise began to take hold.

As I faced the battles in my mind and implemented this essential tool, the battlefield became a place of victory.

- Fact - God's Word stands forever.
- Faith - Put your trust in Him.
- Feelings - Emotions will come into alignment.

March on, Warrior, and get in step with "Fact - Faith – Feelings" and watch destructive thought patterns go!

EITHER YOU BELIEVE IT... OR YOU DON'T

"We demolish arguments and every pretension that sets itself
up against the knowledge of God, and we take captive every
thought to make it obedient to Christ."
2 Corinthians 10:5 (NIV)

My faith began building in small ways as I made the choice to believe God's Word and what He said about me. I needed weapons of warfare that would pull down the strongholds in my mind. This is why we need God's Word as our plumbline. It will correct us when we get off course.

When we choose to believe God's Word over our feelings, the fruit will be evident. I went from being anxious, fearful, and unstable to being confident in God's Word and what He says about me in scripture. It began to change how I thought, resulting in a healthy, strong emotional life.

It's all about your choice and deciding what you believe. Will you choose to believe God's Word and reap the benefits of good fruit? Or will you choose your feelings and be like a ship tossed to and fro?

The times are critical for us as Warriors to walk in line with God's Word and reap the benefits.

Choose to believe God's Word so we can fight our battles as true Warriors!

Note: I am not implying you stuff your feelings deep down inside and don't allow yourself to feel or acknowledge them. Our emotions are often like a spiritual barometer to alert us if there is a need to reach out and get the help and support, we may require. I personally found additional inner healing through a Sozo Ministry where I learned about how trauma, unforgiveness, lies, and wounds had affected my soul. I encourage you to reach out to a local church for help or you may contact: Bethel Sozo[21] - Bethel Sozo)

QR Code #15: Bethel Sozo

KEEP YOUR FEET MOVING

"Give careful thought to the paths for your feet
and be steadfast in all your ways."
Proverbs 4:26 (NIV)

It's imperative we stand up and be strong when we have to deal with toxic people and situations. Whether that toxic person is a friend, a coworker, or even a family member, this wise strategy was given to me by a counselor—to "keep your feet moving." In other words, when you anticipate a difficult situation or know you will be faced with someone who is toxic or unsafe, you don't want your feet planted there for a long period of time. Have a plan, spend as little time as possible, and move on. Even when you unexpectedly find yourself faced with this type of scenario, think proactively. Say you have another appointment or engagement and keep your feet moving!

Take time to identify the people and situations in your life where you need to "keep your feet moving."

Choose to have a Warrior mindset—prepare and have a plan for when the time comes!

Note: If you have to deal with someone who is potentially dangerous or abusive, please contact your local church, social services, or, if need be, law enforcement.

BOUNDARIES AND GUARDRAILS

"It seems to me that if there is a bad taste in your mouth,
you spit it out. You don't constantly swallow it back."[22]
Barbara Wilberforce, *Amazing Grace*

When your emotions begin to run wild, set boundaries and put-up guardrails. Keep from running off the road and out of control!

Ask yourself, what is causing me to go outside the guardrails? Is it over-commitment, stress, a particular relationship, a health issue, unforgiveness, or unresolved emotional pain?

If you do go out of bounds or outside the guardrails, simply repent, take communion, write a prayer of confession, apologize, forgive, or write to the person who offended you. Then burn it or shred it, just get it out! Seek help if need be. Work it out and find true freedom.

Stay on course, be true to yourself, don't overcommit, and stay within the guardrails.

Ask God for wisdom. Be vigilant as a Warrior, and He will direct your path and show you the way.

ESSENTIAL TOOLS FOR VIBRANT LIVING

Bring Kingdom change through, gratitude, music, books, movies, journaling, and art.

A HEART OF GRATITUDE

"Give thanks in all circumstances; for this is God's will
for you in Christ Jesus."
1 Thessalonians 5:18 (NIV)

There is a spiritual law that God speaks to us through His Word about thankfulness. Something happens when we choose to be thankful.

Being thankful can move you from a victim mentality to a victor mentality. When the soul starts spiraling down or your thoughts begin to go dark, make a choice to be thankful. In the midst of hard things, make a shift. Challenge yourself to think about ten things you are grateful for and write them down. This simple act has the power to shift your thoughts from being hopeless to hopeful.

Choose to have a heart of gratitude. Warrior, seek out things to be grateful for and watch your thoughts shift.

ENGAGING MUSIC, INSPIRING BOOKS, WARRIOR MOVIES

Create an atmosphere that is a conduit to the Holy Spirit—a place where your Warrior Heart can be nurtured, strengthened, and activated. You can change the atmosphere through powerful music, an encouraging book, or an inspiring movie to activate the Warrior within.

Music:

My spirit comes alive with engaging music. This can be deep, worshipful music such as anything by Bethel Music, Julie True, or The Riveras. Also, intense movie theme songs (*The Last of the Mohicans, Braveheart, Lord of the Rings*) or vigorous violin, piano, or cello music by Lindsey Stirling, The Piano Guys, Peter Hollins, or symphonic classical greats like Mozart, Handel, and Beethoven ignite my spirit.

Warrior, move from the doldrums to a vibrant, energetic atmosphere where your creativity will flow!

Recommended Books:
- *An Army Arising*, by Christ John Otto
  Learn why artists are on the front line of the next move of God
- *Born to Create*, by Theresa Dedmon
  The power of the arts for healing, evangelism, and the prophetic
- *Soul Decrees*, by Katie Souza
  When you need healing in your soul (mind, will, and emotions)
- *Handbook to Happiness*, by Charles R. Solomon
  When you want to understand your true identity in Christ
- *Roar From Zion*, by Paul Wilbur
  Discover Jesus in ancient Jewish traditions and the importance of Sabbath rest
- *Writing to the Father* by Jackie Jacobsen
  A power-packed booklet with great teaching on journaling
- *The Dream Giver*, by Bruce Wilkinson
  A beautiful story of how God does indeed want us to live our dreams
- *Crafted Prayer*, by Graham Cooke
  Learn and understand how to craft a prayer effectively
- *The Path*, by Laurie Beth Jones
  How to write a mission statement
- The War of Art, by Steven Pressfield
  How to push past the enemy of resistance in pursuit of your dreams
- *Beholding and Becoming*, by Jerry Coulter
  Know true transformation through intimacy with Jesus Christ

Recommended Movies:
- Braveheart - The courageous story of William Wallace and his cry for freedom!
- *Amazing Grace* - The resolve of William Wilberforce to end the "slave trade"
- *Secretariat* - The true inspirational story of the greatest racehorse of all time
- *Gladiator* - The Roman general who became a slave and brought justice to the throne

- *Wonder Woman* - Superhero film based on DC Comics
- *Joan of Arc* - Starring Leelee Sobieski, excellent portrayal of her battles and life
- *The Darkest Hour* - Winston Churchill, during WWII, led with courage against incredible odds
- *Last of the Mohicans* - Adventure, love, and passion, Colonial War conflict
- *The Hobbit and The Lord of the Rings* – J.R.R. Tolkien's epic adventures of fantasy masterpieces
- The Marvel Movies - Marvel Comics superheroes where good wins over evil

Warrior, what are your go-to Warrior songs, words, and movies?

JOURNALING AND ART

"Art shifts nations."[23] - Theresa Dedmon, *Born to Create*

Journaling and art have the power to grow faith, give hope, and impart courage. Investing time in writing and giving deep thought to God's Word can change your viewpoint to God's perspective and what is possible in life.

Warrior, God wants us to cocreate with Him. It's time to move forward with your passion!

Ideas for Journals and Art:
- Personal - Overcome a bad habit or gain control over your time and money.
- Music - Learn about music or an instrument.
- Physical - Implement a plan to get in shape or prepare for a marathon.
- Art - Do a series on birds or clouds.
- Dreams - Write down your dreams and seek answers to understand them.
- Spiritual - Grow in your faith. Do a study on wisdom.

- Nature - Learn about plants in your area or research national parks to visit.
- Prophetic - Draw or paint a picture referring to word's others have spoken over you.

Benefits of Writing and Art:
- Connects our hearts to God's heart
- Inspires vision
- Gives us a voice
- Incites community
- Enriches our relationships
- Increases our creativity
- Imparts revelation, wisdom, and understanding
- Releases freedom, healing, and joy
- Brings Heaven to Earth through our words and art
- Influences others, communities, and nations with the Kingdom of God

Journal and Art Exercise:
- Start with a single line or the stroke of a brush.
- Don't edit. Just enjoy a creative moment!
- Put on worship music and write or paint.
- Release the problems, challenges, and difficulties of life.
- Embrace this time and receive all God has for you!

Famous people who journaled and combined it with art:
- Leonardo da Vinci - inventor and artist
- Lewis and Clark Expedition - Journaled their journey, documented with drawings
- Thomas Edison - Journaled and made drawings of inventions
- Beatrix Potter – *The Tale of Peter Rabbit*, author and artist

God put you on this Earth for such a time as this, Warrior, so start today to invest in yourself with small, courageous steps that will help lead to a significant change in your life!

QUESTIONS:

1. What short dynamic phrases do you have that keep you moving?

2. What essential tools have you discovered that bring lasting change?

3. On a scale of one to ten, how are you at having a heart of gratitude?

CHAPTER SIX

CREATED TO CREATE

He is resurrection life
He is thunder in my veins
He is the fire in my heart
He is an enduring light in my eyes
His glory is bursting forth in my soul
This is the day I break free in resurrection power!

Warrior, your gift to create is God-given for the purposes of healing, strengthening, and releasing life.

Akiane Kramarik, famous for her painting of Jesus, *Prince of Peace*, painted when she was only eight years old, said, 'Jesus spoke to [me] when [I] was four years old, encouraging [me] to draw and paint [my] visions."[24] Her story is a phenomenal testimony to the power of art and creativity in our lives. You may see her painting in this short clip from the documentary, *Painting the Impossible!*[25]

QR Code #16: Akiane Kramarik
Trailer from Documentary "Painting The Impossible"
by Akiane

THE SECRET ARSENAL OF THE ARTS

What are the arts? God is the originator of all art and all artistic crafts. He is our brilliant Creator God who formed and made everything. Beauty is clearly seen in His creation and all of nature. In Genesis 1, we see six days of God's creation come into being:

> "In the beginning, God created the heavens and the earth."
> Genesis 1:1 (NIV)

Each day while creating the universe, God speaks the Word. This holy vibration manifests light, water, sky, land, and sea; vegetation, plants, and trees; sun, moon, and stars; birds, sea creatures, and land animals. And in utter amazement, we behold as God creates man in His own image.

> "So, God created man in His own image; in the image of God He created him; male and female He created them."
> Genesis 1:27 (ESV)

Therefore, we're made in His image and can co-create with Him.

This was exemplified through the artistic virtues of Bezalel, the master craftsman God chose for fashioning and filling the Tabernacle of God:

> "The LORD has filled Bezalel with the Spirit of God, giving him great wisdom, ability, and expertise in all kinds of crafts."
> Exodus 35:31 (NLT)

Bezalel and his team of expert artists and designers were endowed with all the creativity needed to fashion and furnish the Tabernacle of God. Can you imagine being commissioned to create the Tabernacle of God? This phenomenal divine assignment encompassed everything from bronze, gold, and silver to all kinds of woodwork. This demanded the artistry of "engravers, designers, embroiders and weavers," and vastly more. Every detail, from the tiniest stitch to the massive beams, was to be created with perfect precision to house the presence of our Creator God!

Creativity can be seen in God's DNA flowing triumphantly in human history through the masterful design and extraordinary creations of artists with all different types of expression.

My Warrior Heart was stirred while in Italy when walking the perimeters of the Coliseum, looking with wonder at the Leaning Tower of Pisa, awestruck as I viewed Michelangelo's stunning artwork on the ceiling of the Sistine Chapel.

Riverdance[26] is another display of God's extraordinary gift of mastery. Irish culture comes to life in this exhilarating theatrical performance of explosive artistry, glorious music, and robust dancers who move like Warriors in unison with thunderous military steps.

QR Code #17: Riverdance
Riverdance The New 25th Anniversary Show

The immensity of how the arts can be expressed and their many facets is boundless.

To see a more extensive representation of what the arts include, check out my list here.

QR Code #18: List of the Arts

HOW DOES GOD SPEAK THROUGH ART?

JOURNAL THE FATHER'S HEART

"And because we are his children, God has sent the Spirit of his Son
into our hearts, prompting us to call out, 'Abba, Father.'"
Galatians 4:6 (NLT)

Journaling holds great value and huge potential to change lives, nations,
and the world.

As in the book of Acts, Christians can turn this world upside down. We
need to know the Father's heart and who we are as His family, joined as
one in the Body of Christ.

Warrior, let's join and work together as an army of artists and be world
changers for God's glory!

DANCE BRINGS JOY AND HEALING

"Praise until you worship, and worship until the glory falls!"[27]
Ruth Ward Heflin, *Glory: Experiencing the Atmosphere of Heaven*

My entire body, soul, and spirit are engaged when I dance. As I step into
an atmosphere of Heaven where God's glory resides, it's a place like none
other—honorable, majestic, and holy. Here, I have found profound healing
in God's presence as I give Him my all. The power of God changes me
through worship.

With eyes closed, I wait for the divine exchange of the Holy Spirit.
At that moment, I feel His presence, deep love, affirmation, and complete
acceptance of me. I partake in an intimate, passionate, two-way relationship as true lovers coming together.

"But the time is coming—indeed it's here now—when true worshipers will worship the Father in spirit and in truth. The Father is looking for those who will worship him that way." John 4:23 (NLT)

God seeks those who will worship Him in spirit and in truth.

Warrior, won't you join me? Will you embrace a life of worship and creative passions God has placed in you?

QR Code #19: Dance Flags

PAINT THE REALITY OF THE SPIRIT REALM

"Creative expression can not only enhance the
Kingdom message but can embody it."[28]
Theresa Dedmon, *Born to Create*

Through the arts, God becomes more real. I have grown, my life has deepened, and I have found my voice. Additionally, the arts have healed my heart through inspired drawings that testify to the battles won.

There are many effective ways to reach others with life-changing art, poetry, and testimonies that vitally impact lives.

When we bring the reality of the spirit realm through art, others can seize the opportunity to be strengthened, healed, and renewed.

It's time, Warrior, to take steps of courage with your creative gifts so the world may know Him who is life!

QR Code #20: Prophetic Art Ch 6

PRAYERS THAT HEAL

"When we craft a prayer, our crisis becomes
an opportunity for God to work."[29]
Graham Cooke, *Crafted Prayer*

The essence of our words and language carries great weight, not only for communicating but for creating. They carry God's anointing when we wield them into prayers that glorify Him. I can see the Father touching every letter of each word we write and each prayer we speak to Him. His *dunamis* power resounds with the vibrations of Heaven, carrying life, hope, and healing to our broken world! My heart is stirred, knowing His Holy Spirit, fire and presence are breathing new life through my prayers.

Write a Healing Prayer:
- Identify the specific purpose of your prayer.
- Invite the Holy Spirit to join you in creating your prayer.
- Write out your request and present it to God.
- Include a relevant Bible verse.
- Conclude with thanksgiving to God.

Example:
Identify - Give a critical message
Invite - Father God, Jesus, and the Holy Spirit
Request - Help me be focused, grounded, and clear-minded as I prepare this important message. Help me to rest in You and break through walls of confusion and striving. I enter where Your Spirit is light and free.
Bible Verse - Then you will experience God's peace, which exceeds anything we can understand. His peace will guard your hearts and minds as you live in Christ Jesus. Philippians 4:7 (NLT)
Conclude - I place my trust in You and thank You for hearing my prayers!

- Now believe that God unquestionably hears your prayers.
- Know that your words carry great weight in the Heavenly realm.
- Trust God to work on your behalf.

Warrior, watch and see your words carry life, hope, and healing for yourself and others!

HOW DOES CREATIVITY BRING HEALING?

"God radically heals through supernatural creativity."[30]
Theresa Dedmon, *Born to Create*

The arts have brought healing into my life mentally, emotionally, and spiritually. A vast amount of proof testifies how writing, or any other form of art brings healing and increases a person's overall well-being.

Science Aspects: *Huff Post 2-13-2015*[31]
1. Increases IQ
2. Improves communication
3. Imparts healing—mental, emotional, and physical
4. Elevates endorphins and dopamine
5. Strengthens neural pathways

Emotional Aspects:
1. Validates our true identity in Him (Colossians 3:12)
2. Develops creativity in us (Exodus 35:31-32)
3. Awakens our gifts (Psalm 45:1)
4. Increases intimacy with God (Psalm 63:1)
5. Brings healing and stability to the Soul (Romans 12:12)

Spiritual Aspects:
1. Experience Heaven touching Earth
2. Divine connection to the Godhead
3. Expresses His life in us
4. Affirms us as God's sons and daughters
5. Moves us past the natural into the supernatural

There are many opportunities to help grow the gifts God has placed in you and for you to identify, pursue, and find people, communities, and organizations that can help champion you.

Warrior, we've grown in our understanding of what the arts are and how they're used to heal, strengthen, and renew.

We're now ready to activate the Warrior within!

QUESTIONS:

1. Describe what the arts mean to you.

2. What difference have they made in your own life?

3. How have you experienced your own healing through the arts?

PART FOUR

ACTIVATE

THE WARRIOR

WITHIN

CHAPTER SEVEN

DISCOVER YOUR

CALLING

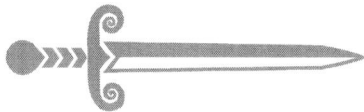

She began to declare:
I am rising above
I am gaining ground
My feet know where they're going
My eyes are focused on Him
I know what I am to do
I will not surrender, back down, or give up
I stay the course of my calling
I know God's will for my life
He is for me
I will not fear
My steps are strong
My faith is growing
I have the victory!

It's time for your Warrior steps to gain ground and your faith to grow in pursuit of your God-given calling. Go forth!

DISCOVER YOUR CALLING

In the 1999 movie *Joan of Arc*,[32] we watch Joan of Arc as a young girl receive divine visitations, and at the young age of seventeen, becomes a Warrior on behalf of France. Her mission was to lead a small army to free France from its long-running war with England and to see the prince crowned King Charles VII. Sadly, Joan was captured by Anglo-Burgundian forces, who had sided with the British, sold her to the English, and then tried her for witchcraft and heresy. She was burned at the stake in 1431, at the age of nineteen. Twenty years after her death, a new trial ordered by the same King Charles VII, cleared her name.

Revealed in the following quote is her Warrior Heart of courage:

> "Every man gives his life for what he believes. Every woman gives her life for what she believes. Sometimes people believe in little or nothing; nevertheless, they give up their lives to that little or nothing. One life is all we have, and we live it as we believe in living it, and then it's gone. But to surrender what you are and live without belief — that's more terrible than dying — more terrible than dying young." [33]

QR Code #21: Joan of Arc
Joan of Arc (1999) - Trailer

One life is all we have. And then it's gone. Are you going to give your life for what you believe?

ACTIVATE THE WARRIOR WITHIN

"Go forward bravely. Fear nothing. Trust in God; all will be well."[34]
Joan of Arc

There is no easy way to access the Warrior within. If that were true, we'd all be Warriors! We must be hungry, determined, and tired of mediocrity to contend for and fight for our destinies. Like Gideon, God will name us and call us out into our true identities in Him, even when we think we're the weakest, most hidden, and least influential person in our clan.

But God will help you truly take hold and believe that you are indeed that "Mighty Man of Valor" or "Braveheart" who has a critical mission to fulfill.

He will get us there if we don't quit, give up, or lose heart. Never surrender! The choice is ours.

Warrior, trust God to guide your steps as He helps to reveal and identify your calling.

IDENTIFY YOUR GIFTS

"God has given each of you a gift from his great variety
of spiritual gifts. Use them well to serve one another."
1 Peter 4:10 (NLT)

Jesus, the Ultimate Warrior, asked the right questions. He knows just how to get to the truth and reveal what's in a person's heart.

Let's start with your relationship with God. Journal the answer to the following questions with intention and purpose. Inquire of the Lord and gain insight into the direction of your calling.

Ask God What He Says About You:
- What do you think of me?
- How do you see me?
- Where can I make the most difference?

- In what ways do you see me being used to serve others?
- What do I have "in my hand" that's available to me now?
- Why am I on this Earth at this time in history?
- Why did You create me and for what?
- Who do you say I am?

Wait on the Lord for His response.
Be assured, Warrior. The Lord hears you and will answer you.

Discover Your People Groups:
- What group of people have your interests, passion, or heart for others?
- What group of people desire to see Kingdom change in the world?
- Who are the influencers and how can you connect with them?
- What group of people are like-minded and making a difference in the world?
- What group of people do you relate to best?
- Which groups have the same goals, outlook, and vision?
- What people make you come alive?
- What groups stir the fire and passion in you?

Warrior, these answers will help you determine the people who will help to bring exponential growth to your life and the lives of others!

Find Your Tribe of Creatives:
- What group of people are bringing creative change that inspires you?
- What creative outreaches enliven you?
- Which creative community projects interest you?
- What group of creative influencers would you like to plug into?
- What groups can benefit from your talents and gifts?
- What organizations, ministries, and businesses express your heart for creativity?
- What creative tribe helps you to grow and challenges you to become your best?

- What would that look like if you could create a tribe of your own?

Warrior, when you connect with your tribe of creatives, there will be no stopping you!

Revisit The Past:
Look back to when you were young. Be insightful.

- What things did you love to do as a child?
- Where were the places you loved to go?
- What were your favorite things in school?
- What did you dream of or imagine you were doing?
- Who did you want to be like?
- What heroes did you have and why?
- What did you want to be when you grew up?
- What were your friends like?

Often you can see the beginnings of a gift, long forgotten, lost in the shuffle, pushed away by a family member or a teacher who discouraged you.
Warrior, it's time to see if any lost treasures can be recovered!

Passion
> "Only God creates. The rest of us just copy."[35]
> Michelangelo

Michelangelo's Sistine Chapel ceiling art eloquently reveals a man's hand reaching out to touch the hand of God. At the point where the fingers touch, a heavenly synergy joins us to Him. The artwork provides powerful imagery of Heaven invading Earth. A heavenly exchange occurs when we connect to God through the arts.
What passion is being stirred in you?
Warrior, it's time to reach out and touch the hand of God to receive the passion He has placed in you!

HOW TO LIVE OUT YOUR CALLING

"We are on the verge of a great awakening — and possibly a
reformation — that will be global in scale…This is the moment
of the artist. It is the moment of the troubadour, the dramatist,
and the designer. It is the moment of the filmmaker, the novelist,
the dancer, the puppeteer, the poet, and the painter. The storytellers
have been set apart for this moment." [36]
Christ John Otto, *An Army Arising: Why Artists are on
the Frontline of the Next Move of God*

We live in unprecedented times and are "on the verge of a great awakening." God is rallying His creatives to step into this moment and fulfill the call on their lives.

Declarations

The Spirit of the Lord is on me because he has anointed me to
proclaim good news to the poor. He has sent me to proclaim
freedom for the prisoners and recovery of sight for the blind,
to set the oppressed free, to proclaim the year of the Lord's favor.
Luke 4:18-19 (NIV)

You can amplify what God has placed in your heart with declarations.

You can speak out your calling through passionate prayer, worship, and warfare.

Declarations are not just wishful thinking or pie-in-the-sky words. These are clear statements and proclamations you have spoken over your life. God tells us directives through His Word or words spoken through trusted leaders in our lives.

These words carry power and authority. Take hold of these words and keep them in the forefront of your mind. Speak them over yourself to build courage and strengthen yourself.

The following is a declaration I created, inspired by Proverbs 13:12 (NIV). "Hope deferred makes the heart sick, but a longing fulfilled is a tree of life."

Reach into Heaven Declaration:

My hope is no longer deferred.

I am a tree of life that has full access to Heaven.

My branches are growing and spreading

Reaching out to the things of God

As I seek him with my

Whole heart, soul, and strength!

As he heals me

My branches begin to burst forth with new life!

My leaves are a beautiful, spring-like, brilliant green.

Fresh, vibrant, and so alive!

Yes, I am a tree of life, whether I feel like it or not.

This is my true identity.

QR CODE #22: Prophetic Artwork Ch 7

I am a champion in the Kingdom of God, called to proclaim the coming revival through writing, worship, art, and prayer.

Revival Declarations:

I am a revivalist

I am a voice for the things of God

I am calling forth the end-time harvest of souls

I am a "Burning One," a flame of God's Holy Fire on the Earth

I am anointed to set those who are bound, free!

I am a mighty messenger for the things of God

I am a braveheart who calls hearts to courage, freedom, and destiny

I am filled with the Holy Spirit for evangelism

I am called to awaken those who are asleep

Heaven is invading me on every level!

Now it's time for you to write, speak out, and see the power of your declarations.

Use key Bible verses God has spoken into your life and make them personal to you. Then put your signature on them and ask God to breathe His breath on them.

Start with ten declarations beginning with the statement, "I am _____!"

I know you can do it, Warrior. What's been hidden in your heart for so long? It's time to speak it out!

See Appendix: Resources on Revival

RISK

This is my command—be strong and courageous! Do not be afraid or discouraged. For the LORD your God is with you wherever you go.
Joshua 1:9 (NLT)

God loves it when we RISK and go beyond our comfort zones.

"Our risk gives God an opportunity to work."[37]
Theresa Dedmon, *Create Without Walls*

When we follow God's lead, gather our courage, and take risks, that's when miracles happen.

Begin by taking one action. One step of courage will start the process. Suggested action steps are:

- Write an encouraging note for someone who is discouraged.
- Check in with a friend and speak words of hope.
- Make that phone call you've been putting off.
- Connect with people who have a similar passion or vision.
- Take a class and grow in an area where you want to "stretch your tent pegs."

- Create a prophetic art piece and give it to the barista at your coffee shop with a word of encouragement. I guarantee it will make their day!

Now is the time to step out of your comfort zone and discover the Warrior God created you to be!

COMMUNITY

"And all the people gathered as one man into the square
before the Water Gate."
Nehemiah 8:1a (ESV)

As you step further into your identity as a creative, you'll begin to see the bigger picture and requisites for community. It is more vital now than ever for the body of Christ to join "as one."

Together we can repair, build, and restore communities, regions, and nations. United, we can move mountains! Let's lock arms, move together "as one," and see what our God can do!

Warrior, identify other Warriors who will join with you "as one" and move mountains!

Now that the Warrior is being activated, let's find ways to avoid becoming apathetic!

QUESTIONS:

1. What makes the Warrior in you come alive?

2. What battleground are you called to where you can make the most difference?

3. Who are the people that call out the Warrior in you?

Note: There are multiple tests you can take online that will help you identify your specific personality traits, spiritual gifts, and leadership qualities, among others.

Resources in Appendix: Tests Online

There are many different personalities, ways, and styles of learning and expressing oneself as a "Warrior" that don't need to be pushed or driven. For example, I am a Type A, goal-oriented personality who likes structure and challenges. However, there is no right or wrong way to engage with the Lord and your gifts as a creative. I want to clarify that I do not intend to pressure any of you. God needs us all, and how he created us individually is honored and welcomed as you engage in the activities and call to action, I have listed in the following chapters. Peace, living from a place of rest, and times of refreshing are just as vitally important. I am here to support you in moving forward in whatever way works for you, in whatever capacity you can.

CHAPTER EIGHT

OVERCOMING

RESISTANCE

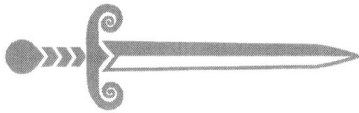

She wondered how many great Warriors fell,
Never to rise again.
She did not want to be a casualty.
This was an enemy camp
There were no rules of engagement
There was no honor,
These were ruthless, heartless, evil rulers
That had no respect for life.
She would not give the enemy the satisfaction anymore
She only wanted to give glory to God
Her King, her Deliverer, her Rescuing Knight.

We have a better chance of survival if we work and stay together! High entertainment during the Roman Empire was watching slaves be killed and eaten alive by wild animals. In the movie *Gladiator*, when former general Maximus (now a slave) and other gladiators are released into the arena, Maximus asks, "Have any of you been in the army? Whatever comes out of these gates, we have a better chance of survival if we work together. Do you understand? If we stay together, we survive."[38]

Suddenly, the gates open. Chariots with Roman Warriors roar into the arena.

Maximus abruptly yells, "Come together. Lock our shields. Stay as one! Hold. As One!"

We watch as every one of the Roman Warriors is annihilated. There's power in unity. The times are critical. Let's come together, lock our shields, and move ahead "as one!"

QR Code #23: Gladiator
Gladiator clip

HOW TO OVERCOME RESISTANCE

How many of us have fallen prey to the enemy of resistance?

In the book *The War of Art*[39] by Steven Presfield, the author discovers a very real battle creatives must face. Its name is "resistance," and it comes in many forms. Resistance does NOT want us to advance or break free from things that hold us back, physically, mentally, or spiritually.

The activities that most commonly elicit resistance are:

- Writing, painting, or any creative art
- An entrepreneurial venture, diet, or health program
- Spiritual advancement or education of any kind

- Any political, moral, or ethical courage
- Endeavors to help others
- Any act that entails commitment of the heart
- Taking a principled stand in the face of adversity

How do we push against the enemy of resistance? We sit down and do the work: we write, we paint, we dance, we sing, and we speak out our passion! Whatever we need to do, we are the world changers, and it will take some hard pushing…as one!

Suggested action steps are:

- Write the letter you've been putting off or the book you know is in you.
- Get your art supplies out of the closet and paint, draw, create.
- Join the choir, or a worship group, and sing.
- Put on your dancing shoes and dance.
- Get your instrument out and start playing, take lessons or join a quartet.
- Be a voice in your community and take a stand for righteousness.

Take action. Just do it!

I know the Warrior in you can. Once you do, you won't want to stop!

FOCUS

"We must regain our focus daily."[40]
Author Unknown

To regain our focus daily, we must be vigilant. With all of the demands of life, the struggle is real. To follow our dreams and become the Warrior we know is inside us, we must awaken the fire of our passion through intimate time with God, purposeful thinking, and writing with intention…as one!

- Keep a daily prayer journal you refer to as you grow in your relationship with the Lord.

- Get a weekly planner to assist in organizing your week, schedule, and priorities.
- Join a mastermind group of like-minded people to push you in reaching goals, ideas, and dreams.
- Invest in a mentor, coach, or teacher to support you in business, ministry, or an artistic endeavor.
- Find an accountability partner or group that will aid you in following through on your goals.

Warrior, it's critical we spend time with God, know His will for us, and walk in it.

HAMMER VERSES

"'Does not My word burn like fire?' says the Lord, 'Is it not like a mighty hammer that smashes a rock to pieces?'"
Jeremiah 23:29 (NLT)

His word became a sword, a hammer that shattered the rocks in my life.

His promises, when spoken over and over again, renewed my mind, set me free, and gave me the authority to speak to mountains.

What are hammer verses?

- These are scripture verses that help you to stand on the battlefield.
- These are words that anchor your soul.
- These verses crush the enemy's head.
- They silence the lying tongue.
- These scriptures bring life back into your spiritual lungs.

Warrior, now is the time to get your spiritual hammer out and strike back…as one!

Write out your hammer verses. Speak them out, cry them out, and shout them out. Get them out into the atmosphere. Rally your Warrior Heart and become immovable!

Seven hammer verses that give you the courage to stand, shatter rocks, rejoice in trials, ignite a fire inside, break through hopelessness, push back the darkness, and train your hands for war:

1. …Then after the battle, you will still be standing firm.
   Ephesians 6:13 (NLT)
2. "Does not My word burn like fire?" says the Lord, "Is it not like a mighty hammer that smashes a rock to pieces?"
   Jeremiah 23:29 (NLT)
3. Though the fig tree does not bud and there are no grapes on the vines…I will be joyful in God my Savior.
   Habakkuk 3:17-18 (NIV)
4. …His word is in my heart like a fire, a fire shut up in my bones.
   Jeremiah 20:9 (NIV)
5. Why am I discouraged? Why is my heart so sad?
   Psalm 43:5 (NLT)
6. No weapon forged against you will prevail…
   Isaiah 54:17 (NIV)
7. Praise be to the Lord my Rock, who trains my hands for war, my fingers for battle.
   Psalm 144:1 (NIV)

So, tell me, Warrior, what are your hammer verses?

QR Code #24: 100 Promises of God

TAKE UP YOUR SWORD

"This is the moment for the artist to arise. This is the moment
for the artist to make a way. This is the moment for the artist
to be the sermon. This is the day for the artisan to be revealed
and declare the glory of God."[41]
Christ John Otto, *An Army Arising: Why Artists
are on the Frontlines of the Next Move of God*

The arts are a sword we can wield to reach those from all different back-
grounds, cultures, beliefs, and levels of abuse or trauma. God works power-
fully through the arts to set the captives free.

This is indeed the moment of the artist, storyteller, and voice that makes
a difference in the world…as one!

Identify ways to express the arts in your areas of influence; to declare
and reveal the glory of God.

Our Warrior God is calling us to create and move forward with brave
acts of courage!

PASSIONATE PRAYERS

"…The prayer of a righteous person is powerful and effective."
James 5:16b (NIV)

God hears our prayers and affirms that the "prayer of a righteous person is
powerful and effective."

We either believe Him, or we don't! Prayer does indeed change things.
We see evidence of this in the following verses:

Jesus heals Jairus's daughter - Mark 5:23
Peter is released from prison - Acts 12:5-7
Hannah prays for a son - 1 Samuel 1:11
Moses prays to see God's glory - Exodus 33:18

Elisha prays for his servant's eyes to be open to an unseen vast army - 2 Kings 6:17

There are many ways we can express our prayers and entreat God to intercede, to bring an atmosphere of hope, change, and victory through our worship, dance, writing, and the arts…as one!

- Worship - Dance before the Lord to bring breakthrough.
- Write - Be specific as to your request. Include hammer verses. Be passionate.
- The Arts - Create a prophetic art piece. Write or sing a song for healing.

Warrior, watch and see your passionate prayers carry life, hope, and healing for others and the things you are believing for.

PROPHETIC ARTS

"For behold, darkness will cover the earth,
And deep darkness the peoples; But the LORD
will rise upon you, And His glory will appear upon you."
Isaiah 60:2 (NASB)

In Isaiah, we see the transformation of darkness into light. This is God's way.

When I draw or paint, I enter into a prophetic mindset where I can create images of myself or others being ministered to, breaking through, overcoming, rejoicing, being victorious, brave, and courageous.

These images carry the touch of the Master Artist, our Creator God, who can bring great freedom. In a sense, I am creating the world I am determined to step into, from darkness to light and deep darkness to glory…as one!

- What opposition are you facing?
- Give voice to it with your words, art, dance, or declarations.

- From God's perspective, activate the prophetic in your life through creative expression.

Warrior, I can see this prophetic gift growing inside of you!

RISK

"If you hear a voice within you say, 'you cannot paint,'
then by all means paint, and that voice will be silenced."[42]
Vincent Van Gogh

We risk when we decide to step onto the battlefield. Whether it be at the grocery store, in a meeting, or with family, there are many opportunities to step out.

These acts of courage, no matter how small, can move you from complacency and awaken the Warrior within and in others…as one!

Suggested ways to take risks:

- Create an art piece; through painting, writing an encouraging word, or a photograph. Ask God who He wants to receive it.
- Think of places you go to often. Who might need a word of encouragement?
- Be the "cup of water" to a thirsty world, whether it's people at work, the gym, or the coffee shop.
- Be prepared and be intentional.

A great way to prepare for reaching out to others is by creating a "Warrior Outreach Pack" with prophetic artwork, notes of courage, and tracts to give out that speak God's Warrior Words over those who come across your path or that God puts on your heart.

QR Code #25: Warrior Outreach Pack

Let's join together "as one!" and watch as others are transformed and changed by the power of the Holy Spirit!

TIMING

"Who through faith conquered kingdoms, administered justice, and gained what was promised; who shut the mouths of lions, quenched the raging fire, and escaped the edge of the sword; who gained strength from weakness, became mighty in battle, and put foreign armies to flight!"
Hebrews 11:33-34 (NIV)

It's important to prayerfully consider the timing of things. God answers our prayers in many different ways. In Hebrews 11 we see a rich display of God's people overcoming by faith who were: "warned, later received, saw from afar, were enabled, looked forward to, longed for, persevered and endured."

These testimonies of faith give us an understanding of God's wisdom and timing in our lives. What courage we see as these Warriors conquer, administer, overthrow, gain, shut, quench, escape, and become mighty…as one!

Evaluate God's timing in your own life and your faith in God to answer prayer:

- Consider the past twelve to twenty-four months when you were seeking God for answers.
- Create a timeline.
- Write down prayers that have been answered and those that have yet to be answered.
- Trust and wait on Him to bring forth the promises.

Warrior, God is for you. He sees your courage and knows the appointed time!

COURAGE AND BRAVERY

"We conquer by continuing."[44]
George Matheson, Scottish Minister

In certain seasons of our lives, just getting up and brushing our teeth is an act of courage. Putting one foot in front of the other and taking the next step can be a brave thing to do. It can be small, or it can be big. God doesn't waste any of our efforts. He loves to see courage and bravery rise up in us. He is our Brave Warrior calling out the courage in us to take the next step...as one!

How courageous have you been? Let's do an assessment:

• Identify things in your life that take courage and make a plan. Ask God for strategies.
• Write down times you have been brave and how you overcame. What was it like?

The Warrior in you is getting stronger, take up your courage and fight!

WISDOM AND UNDERSTANDING

"For the Lord gives wisdom; from his mouth come knowledge and understanding."
Proverbs 2:6 (NIV)

Proverbs are full of God's wisdom and understanding. Study God's Word in the Proverbs. Take a serious look and identify what currently has "life" and see "what's in your hand" that's available for you to use now?

God has the answers. We just need to ask the hard questions and seek His face...as one!

Suggested action steps:

• Commit to reading one chapter of Proverbs every day.

- Do a study on wisdom.
- Ask God the hard questions and write the answers in your journal.
- To be a great Warrior you need to seek God for His wisdom and understanding. This will bring victory to the battlefields of your life!

Warrior, we are becoming well-equipped, armed with courage and bravery, wisdom and understanding. Let's move on to cast the vision God has imparted to us!

QUESTIONS:

1. What do you do when you hit the wall of resistance?

2. Ask God for new strategies to break through your challenges.

3. How can you boldly move forward to overcome and conquer?

CHAPTER NINE

CAST THE VISION

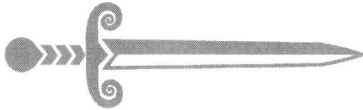

Hope was seen on the horizon.
Joy flickered in the atmosphere,
Signs of change, like springtime,
Began to break through
The hardened ground of her soul.
Her voice of belief spoke into the darkness
And her faith began to grow.
She was no longer the same person,
Much has changed over those years of struggle.
She saw things with new eyes.
The atmosphere around her
Crackled with creativity,
They started to fill her thoughts
And be seen in her dreams…

Dance, on Warrior. It's time to write your mission and cast your vision. ADVANCE!

DOES GOD REALLY WANT ME TO DREAM?

"I will fight for those who cannot fight for themselves."[44]
Wonder Woman

In the movie *Wonder Woman: 1984*,[45] we see a little girl who dreams of being a Warrior.

Trained by the best Warriors of the Amazon, she has a call on her life to fight for the good of mankind.

QR Code #26: Wonder Woman: 1984
Amazon's Olympics Scene | Wonder Woman WW84

Isn't that what God is calling us to do with our creative gifts? We, too, are being trained by the best!

God, our Mighty Warrior, has given us our true identity in Jesus Christ and filled us with His Holy Spirit. We can go out and do virtuous exploits with Him as we fulfill our destiny!

WRITE THE VISION

"Then the LORD answered me and said: 'Write the vision and make it plain on tablets, so he may run who reads it.'"
Habakkuk 2:2 (ESV)

Just as the Lord encouraged Habakkuk to have a written plan, He desires for us to know our purpose and envision what fulfilling that purpose looks like. A strong mission statement and vision statement can play a pivotal role in helping you stay on track to fulfill your God-given purpose.

Specifically, a mission statement describes what you want to do now, whereas a vision statement inspires and motivates what you want to see in the future.

In the book, *The Path: Creating Your Mission Statement for Work and for Life*[46] by Laurie Beth Jones, I discovered the essentials and step-by-step strategies to write my mission over twenty years ago: "I am a Braveheart who calls hearts to a life of freedom, purpose, and destiny in Christ Jesus."

In her book, Jones gives three elements to a good mission statement:

- A mission statement should be no more than a single sentence long.
- It should be easily understood by a twelve-year-old.
- It should be able to be recited by memory at gunpoint. (Soldiers WWII)

Mission Statements in History:

> Jesus - Seek and Save the Lost
> Nehemiah - Rebuild the Walls of Jerusalem
> Joan of Arc - Free France
> Abraham Lincoln - To Preserve the Union
> FDR - End the Depression
> Martin Luther King - Create a Beloved Community
> Mother Teresa - Show Mercy and Compassion to the Dying

As you can see, each of the above examples are focused on community and achieving honorable results "as one!" (From "The Path," page 63) To begin developing your personal mission and vision statements, let's get started:

- Write down three verbs that describe you.
- What are your core values and strong beliefs?
- Identify your people group (homeless, elderly, children, etc.)
- What or who do you have a burden for?
- What makes you come alive?

I am a _____, that _____ to _____ , _____ , _____ .
(Simplified)

Example - (My Personal Mission Statement and Vision)
   Mission: I am a Braveheart who calls hearts to a life of freedom, purpose, and destiny.
   Vision: Raise Up an Army of Courageous Kingdom Influencers

Remember, "Your mission is always bigger than your current role."[47] Laurie Beth Jones

Warrior, speak about your vision so others can catch it and join you in your mission.

MAKE A PLAN

"We can make our plans, but the LORD determines our steps."
Proverbs 16:9 (NLT)

Let's roll out the map to your vision! Use your five senses and engage yourself in it!

Map it out. Vision board it. Journal it. Speak it. Tell others about it!

Creative ways to breathe life into your mission and vision:

1. Vision Board - Create a vision board, put it in picture form, and bring it to life.

"Surrounding yourself with images of your vision causes your
dream to become more alive inside you. It is a vital component
of your success that you surround yourself with what 'can be' and
not just 'what is.' That's the power of vision."[48]
Terri Savelle Foy, *Dream it. Pin it. Live it. Make Vision Boards Work for You*

QR Code #27 - Dream Board Class
Dream Board Class

2. Ask yourself, "What would the most amazing year of my life look like?"
3. Set SMART Goals in the five areas of your life:

1.	Specific	1.	Spiritual
2.	Measurable	2.	Physical
3.	Achievable	3.	Personal
4.	Relevant	4.	Business
5.	Achievable	5.	Passion

4. Ask yourself, "If I only had six months to live..." This will create an urgency to help prioritize what's important in your life.

Smart Goals for Dance: (Example)

Specific - Grow my understanding of dance through God's Word, the books *Glory: Experiencing the Atmosphere of Heaven*[49] by Ruth Ward Heflin and Wielding Banners 50 by David Stanfield

Measurable - Outline how I will grow my understanding.

Achievable - Five Points:
1. When: June 1
2. What: Journal three to five times a week, what I learned, insights, applications
3. Where: Mornings, 7 to 8 a.m.
4. Why: To deepen my understanding and experience of dance
5. How: I will identify six key components of dance and worship

Relevant - What God is doing in this moment through dance and worship

Time - Stamped - Complete by September 1st

It's vital as a Warrior to endure and do the hard work to fulfill your life's mission.

BE EQUIPPED

"In his grace, God has given us different gifts
for doing certain things well."
Romans 12:6 (NLT)

God has given me gifts. I have learned to grow these gifts in unconventional ways. My time with God is paramount. Through the infilling and direction of the Holy Spirit, I can create a world that believes in the impossible. God has sent notable people into my life to help me along the way.

Whether writing, dancing, creating or praying, this is where I grow strong and become equipped.

These are some ways you can grow strong and become equipped, too.

1. Journal - This is where you can fight your battles well!
2. Worship - Pick up your sword. Get a silk flag and dance.
3. Drawing and art - Create images that help you see from Heaven's perspective.
4. Prayer - Hold your ground and believe by faith!

And let's not forget the strength of community…as one!

The following are just a few strategies to help you get started:

• Identify what skills (education, training, experience) you need to advance your vision.

- Find key people to join you in your life's mission.
- Identify places where you can speak about your passion.
- Cast your vision so others can catch it and run with you.
- Seek out essential groups that are like-minded.

Warriors, invest in yourself, seek ways to maximize your skills, and sharpen your swords to acquire excellence!

STAND UP AND BE A VOICE

"I am not afraid; I was born to do this."[51]
Joan of Arc

You have been given a voice. When you speak, be intentional with your words. Be motivated by the mission God has given you. Your voice can be heard and seen in intercession, prophetic art, passionate worship, and by taking action.

Identify places where your voice matters and can make a difference...as one!

To get started, reflect on the following questions:

- What actions can you take to bring positive change?
- Where can you be a voice for the things of God?
- Where can your voice make a difference?
- How can your voice become louder?
- Who do you know that has influence in your community?
- How can you support others and be a voice for the
  Kingdom of God?

Warrior, stand up and know that what you do, matters. You make a difference!

A great way to begin doing so is to make declarations to call forth and strengthen your Warrior voice.

Ten Warrior Voice Declarations:

1. I voice the Word of God.
2. I speak words of life and love with my voice.
3. I speak with confidence.
4. I speak with authority.
5. I pray for God's anointing on my voice.
6. I storm the gates of hell with my voice.
7. My voice moves mountains.
8. I lay my requests before God with my voice.
9. I cry out to God with my voice.
10. I praise God with my voice.

I know the Warrior in you has a voice others need to hear. Now go forward and create your own Warrior voice declarations!

USE THE ARTS AS A VISUAL

"In every block of marble, I see a statue as plain as though it
stood before me, shaped and perfect in attitude and action.
I have only to hew away the rough walls that imprison the
lovely apparition to reveal it to the other eyes as mine see it."[52]
Michelangelo

What an exciting time to be alive! The vision that God has placed in us has a new priority. The importance of our creative work in the world today is becoming urgent. Many of us have prayed, struggled, failed, believed, lost hope, and wondered when this next move of God would be.

I believe that time is now.

Art has the power to move people, cultures, and nations in a remarkable way. Now is the time to become vigilant. Take your position as an artisan and use it as a weapon to fight for the Kingdom of God… as one!

Following are a few questions for consideration:

- What are you believing for?
- What piece of marble do you see that needs the rough wall hewn away?
- Do you see the importance of your work? Why or why not?
- Imagine your creative gift changing the lives of those around you.
- What would that look like?
- What would happen if we went out like Warriors to bring Kingdom-change to the world through our creativity?

Believe with renewed hope, Warrior. You can reach those who hunger and thirst for true life!

BUILD A TEAM OF WARRIORS

"And he said to them, 'Follow me, and I will make you fishers of men.'"
Matthew 4:19 (ESV)

Jesus invited His twelve disciples to follow Him, and they did.
I encourage you to also seek out Warriors who are passionate, like-minded, and supportive of your mission…as one!

Specific action steps:

- Invite other Warriors to join you on your mission.
- Surround yourself with Warriors who will encourage you.
- Discover other Warriors who will call out your best.
- Warriors need other Warriors to rally around them!

Warrior, it's time to build a strong team of Warriors to help carry out your mission!

PROPHETIC WORDS

"But the one who prophesies speaks to people for
their strengthening, encouraging and comfort."
1 Corinthians 14:3 (NIV)

Prophetic words should "edify, encourage, and comfort."

Just like the Prophets of old, God wants us to listen and take heed to what He is saying. Value the prophetic words God has spoken over you through scripture as well as the prophetic words trustworthy people have spoken over you…as one!

Ways to get started:

- Create a prophetic word notebook.
- Gather prophetic words that have been spoken over you.
- Keep them at the forefront of your mind.
- Believe the promises God has given you through these words.

Believe these words, Warrior. Keep them at the forefront of your mind to encourage, edify, and comfort you. Be exhilarated as you begin to implement your plan and march forward!

QUESTIONS:

1. Have you discovered your mission and vision?

2. Have you found your voice?

3. To what and to whom have you been called?

PART FIVE

CONCLUSION

CHAPTER TEN

THE WARRIOR DANCE

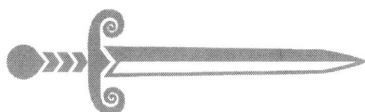

He knew the Warrior Anointing she carried
He saw the fire in her heart
That would rise up with such great
Courage, bravery, and determination
He had placed it there
To bring His ultimate plan of glory.
She would learn His battle plan
For release and glorious freedom
She would burst through the prison doors
A new Warrior, a spiritual soldier
That only He knew was inside her
To bring her out of captivity into victory!

Warrior, as we stand together on the battlefield and survey the landscape before us, we see with new eyes. We are becoming spiritual soldiers, equipped with the essentials to overcome.

It's time to burst through the prison doors to your destiny! You are a Mighty Warrior. Now, stay the course!

COURAGE AND BRAVERY

"This is my command—be strong and courageous! Do not be afraid or discouraged. For the LORD your God is with you wherever you go."
Joshua 1:9 (NLT)

Anytime we take a step toward our dreams, it takes courage. There will always be obstacles, resistance, and pushback. What are you going to do about it? How will you push through, press on, and move forward into not just thinking about it but living the life of a Warrior?

Take ground. Occupy. Believe! You don't have to conquer a mountain every day, but keep moving forward, one step at a time.

Remember: God doesn't waste any of your steps in life. He loves to see courage and bravery rise up in you. He is your Brave Warrior calling out the courage in you to take the next step and burst through the prison doors!

LIVE FROM IDENTITY

"Our identity, based on who we are in Christ, is claimed by faith. We exchange our fleshly identity for the Christ-life, by exchanging a life of defeat for a life of victory."[53]
Dr. Charles R. Solomon, *Handbook to Happiness*

My world was turned upside down when God revealed my true identity in Him. I have never been the same. He proves to me over and over again His faithfulness and affirms me as His daughter. The more I spend time with Him, the more I come alive in who I am in Him.

He has given me life. My heart is set intensely on Him.

Remember: You have been given a new identity in Christ. Your past no longer limits you. Jesus Christ has given you all and more than you need to live a life of abundance. With no limits and no boundaries, you can reach far into the vast riches of Him, who is life…the Giver of Life who is eternal, all-knowing, ever-present, breathing life into you as His Creative Warrior!

STAY IN THE WORD

"In the beginning was the Word, and the Word was with God,
and the Word was God."
John 1:1 (NIV)

God's Word is the compass to our dreams. It keeps us on the path God created for us—an armament to overcome the flesh, the world's influence, and the enemy that can deceive, distract, and defy you from living out God's purpose for your life.

You must contend. Freedom comes at a great cost.

There is a fierce *War of Art* occurring, and you are part of the *Army that is Arising*!

Remember: In order to push back on the strong influence of your flesh, the world, and the enemy, you must change the way you think! One crucial way this happens is to be transformed by God's Word.

WISDOM AND UNDERSTANDING

"For by wise guidance you can wage your war, and in
abundance of counselors there is victory."
Proverbs 24:6 (ESV)

The Bible is full of wisdom and understanding. King Solomon asked God for wisdom and understanding, giving us the book of Proverbs. These testimonies help us on our journey as Warriors to take a serious look at God's Word and seek His wisdom for our lives.

Remember: God has the answers, and as His Warriors, we need to ask the hard questions and seek His face.

BE A VOICE

"I saw the angel in the marble and carved until I set him free."[54]
Michelangelo

You have been given a voice. Be intentional and wield your words for God's glory when you speak. Be motivated by the mission and vision God has given you. Do this through words of courage, prophetic art, and Kingdom messages that inspire.

Remember: Your voice makes a difference! Your voice can be heard in written words, through the arts, demonstrated in dance, worshipful acts, passionate prayer, heartfelt declarations, and immeasurably more. Wield your creative gifts to shine the light of God's Glory!

CREATE A TEAM

"After they prayed, the place where they were meeting was shaken. And they were all filled with the Holy Spirit and spoke the word of God boldly. All the believers were one in heart and mind..."
Acts 4:31-32 (NIV)

Be purposeful in the people who are part of your inner circle of friends. Surround yourself with those Warriors who are there for you, no matter what, who will offer sound wisdom, advice, and a listening ear. You want

Warriors who love you unconditionally, hold you accountable, and challenge you to be your best!

Remember: It's important for Warriors to have another team of Warriors around them. Make sure you get the right ones who are passionate, like-minded, and supportive of your creative gift.

RISK

"Faith is spelled R-I-S-K."[55]
Theresa Dedmon, *Born to Create*

It takes courage to take risks, but God always honors us stepping out in faith. When we take action, this is when He can work, not only in us but in other people. With intention, over time, stepping out in faith will become a lifestyle.

In daily life, be prepared to impart courage, hope, and healing to others as God directs.

Remember: It's in your spiritual DNA to reach out to those in need— the poor, the widows, and others in your community. God's Word directs us to be His Light to the World!

HIS TIMING

"Now faith is confidence in what we hope for and
assurance of what we do not see."
Hebrews 11:1 (NIV)

These testimonies of great faith give wisdom regarding the timing in our own lives.

God answers our prayers, and we overcome by faith as we see from afar, persevere, and endure. What courage and faith those ancient Warriors had!

As Hebrews 11 states, they "conquered, administered, overthrew, gained, shut, quenched, escaped, and became mighty!"

Remember: Our Warrior God is for you and the promises He has placed in your Warrior Heart. Trust and wait on Him to bring them forth. He sees your courage and knows their appointed time!

QUESTIONS:

1. What does your Warrior Dance look like? Describe it. Feel it. See it. Own it!

2. What "act of courage" can you take today and commit to often?

3. Who are you? Who does God say you are? Describe it.

CONCLUSION AND CALL-TO-ACTION

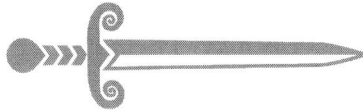

"Arise, shine, for your light has come, and the glory of the Lord rises upon you. See, darkness covers the earth and thick darkness is over the peoples, but the Lord rises upon you and his glory appears over you."
Isaiah 60: 1-2 (NIV)

You have seen how my Warrior God has taken me from deep darkness into His glorious light!

I've grown and overcome through my life's expression in journaling, drawing, art, dance, worship, and prayer. I am becoming the Warrior whom God has created me to be!

This is the way of the Warrior's Dance!

If you want to follow me on this path of overcoming and victory, let's go! Pick up your swords of writing, art, worship, dance, passionate prayer, and creative acts of courage, and join me on the battlefield.

Warrior, there's a brave heart in you. Now believe it!
Let's run our race with courage and see what our Warrior God can do!
I believe in you! Strength, honor and courage, onward…as one!

In the movie *Secretariat*,[56] Penny tells Secretariat to *run his race*. Now it's time to run yours!

QR Code #28: Secretariat
SECRETARIAT - He Laughs At Fear, Afraid of Nothing - (Movie)

Want to connect further? Join my "Women of Courage" movement!
www.DesertThunderArts.com

ACKNOWLEDGMENTS

Special thanks to my content editor, JP Brooks, who coached me like a true Warrior: directing, guiding, and calling out the courage in me to do my best writing. JP gave me insights, strategies, and techniques to slash my way through the fluff in my original manuscript. He helped me eliminate 10,000 words, thus rescuing me from delivering a mediocre story to (what I hope is) a vibrant and compelling script. I'd have him spar against the best, any day!

To my friend, Chris Tracy, who *awakened* the Warrior in me. Through divine connection, God put us together to *run our race*! You have been my teacher, cheerleader, and guide as we venture on this road of life to our dreams! I am eternally grateful to you as we watch them unfold!

Women of Courage who cheered me on along the way:

> Chris, Cindy, Deb, Dara, Sally, Linda S, Vanessa, Lorna, Holly, Joy, Kanda, Harriet, and Merry.
>
> Create Academy Small Group: Pamela, Kris, Linda L, Ileen, and Gail.
>
> My Evergreen friends: Karen, Sally, Rhonda, and Candy.
>
> My Grand Junction adventures group: Angie, Julie, Janice, Pam, and Kathy.
>
> You all held my arms up as I grew weary and repeatedly called out the Warrior in me!

Special thanks to the following teachers, mentors, and coaches in my life:

AAP - Jeremy Brown, Alle Byeseda, and Mike Owens

Create Academy - Theresa Dedmon, Karen Ladage, and Randy Schimon

An Army Arising - Christ John Otto

It's Supernatural!™ - Sid Roth

Paul Wilbur Ministries - Music: Shalom Jerusalem, Jerusalem Arise! Book: *Roar from Zion!*

Mario Murillo - Books: *Vessels of Fire and Glory and Do Not Leave Quietly*

Book Cover - Ooh Snap Photo Booth and Photography by Rachel Romero

Dress by California Costume Collections, Inc., Sword of Eowyn by United Cutlery

NOTES

CHAPTER ONE

1. Warrior. Merriam-Webster.com. Accessed October 23, 2022.
   https://www.merriam-webster.com/dictionary/warrior
2. Warrior. Websters1913.com. Accessed October 23, 2022.
   https://www.websters1913.com/words/Warrior
3. Gibson, Mel, *Braveheart*. United States: Paramount Pictures,
   1995, YouTube movie video, 02.33. Accessed October 23, 2022.
   https://www.youtube.com/watch?v=G4Ym9zokSZo

CHAPTER TWO

4. An Alliance Release, New Line Cinema presents a Wingnut
   Films production; producers, Barrie M. Osborne, Fran Walsh,
   Peter Jackson; screenplay by Fran Walsh & Philippa Boyens &
   Stephen Sinclair & Peter Jackson; directed by Peter Jackson,
   The Lord of the Rings. The Two Towers. [California]: Montréal:
   New Line Home Entertainment; Distributed by Alliance films,
   2011, YouTube movie video 01:26. Accessed October 23, 2022.
   https://www.youtube.com/watch?v=HWHjhRuRoZU

5. Mann, Michael. *The Last of the Mohicans*. United States: Twentieth Century Fox, 1992, YouTube movie video, 02:42. Accessed October 23, 2022. https://www.youtube.com/watch?v=k2edI8Gu6k8

CHAPTER THREE

6. Ritt, Martin, Tamara Asseyev, Alexandra Rose, Irving Ravetch, Harriet Frank, John A. Alonzo, Sidney Levin, et al. 2001, *Norma Rae*. Beverly Hills, Calif: Twentieth Century Fox Home Entertainment, YouTube movie video, 05:26. https://www.youtube.com/watch?v=X8ulYIVcCeY
7. Corrie Ten Boom, *Amazing Love: True Stories of Forgiveness*, Fort Washington, Pa.: Christian Literature, Crusade, 1971.
8. Zhang, Mark, *The Silent Scream*, by Bernard Nathanson, Crusade for Life, and American Portrait Films, 1984.
9. Charles R. Solomon, *Handbook to Happiness*, (Wheaton, IL: Tyndale House, 2011).
10. Charles R Solomon, *Handbook to Happiness*, (Wheaton, IL: Tyndale House, 2011). (*The Wheel and Line - Chapter 2*)
11. Paine, Valerie. "I Am In Christ," YouTube educational video, 01:36. Accessed August 10, 2022. https://www.youtube.com/watch?v=DVN5IDaSD9I

CHAPTER FOUR

12. Jenkins, Patty. *Wonder Woman*. United States: Warner Bros, 2017, YouTube movie video, 02:40. Accessed October 23, 2022. https://www.youtube.com/watch?v=-DwqWu4XOOA
13. Tactics. Vdict.pro. Accessed August 25, 2022. https://vdict.pro/en-en/tactics
14. Decree. Vdict.pro. Accessed August 25, 2022. https://vdict.pro/en-en/decree

15. Luther, Martin. AZQuotes.com. Accessed August 8, 2022. https://www.azquotes.com/quote/365996

16. Jackie Jacobsen, *Writing to the Father*. Self-published, 1996. LedByTheSpiritSchool.org. Accessed October 23, 2022. https://ledbythespiritschool.org/product/writing-to-the-father/

17. Wilbur, Paul. "Jerusalem Arise." YouTube music video, 57:10. Accessed August 12, 2022. https://www.youtube.com/watch?v=bhuvTmlBAeQ

18. Tommey, Matt. "What is Prophetic Art?" MattTommeyMentoring.com. Accessed August 12, 2022. https://www.matttommeymentoring.com/what-is-prophetic-art.html

19. Kimberly and Alberto Rivera. "Royalty". YouTube music video, 07:38. Accessed August 25, 2022. https://www.youtube.com/watch?v=M93pa-F-z10

CHAPTER FIVE

20. Apted, Michael, *Amazing Grace*. United States: Roadside Attractions, 2006, 01:39. Accessed October 23, 2022. https://www.youtube.com/watch?v=o9uwaR_thrc

21. DeSilva, Dawna. BethelSozo.com. Inner Healing and Deliverance Ministry. Accessed October 23, 2022. https://www.bethelsozo.com

22. Wilberforce, Barbara. MovieQuoteDB.com. Accessed August 10, 2022. https://www.moviequotedb.com/movies/amazing-grace-2006/character_2766.html

23. Theresa Dedmon, *Born to Create: Stepping Into Your Supernatural Destiny* (Destiny Image Publishers, April 1, 2012).

CHAPTER SIX

24. Akiane Kramarik, *Akiane: Her Life, Her Art, Her Poetry*, (Nashville, Tenn.: W Publishing Group, c2006).

25. Kramarik, Akiane. Trailer from the Documentary "Painting the Impossible" by Akiane. YouTube video, 01:01. Accessed August 12, 2022. https://www.youtube.com/watch?v=chA3A7Wcshc

26. Riverdance: Composed by Bill Whelan; produced by Moya Doherty; directed by John McColgan. YouTube video, 01:00. Accessed August 12, 2022. https://www.youtube.com/watch?v=r-20mhtICf0
"Riverdance is a theatrical show that consists of mostly Irish music and dance." Accessed October 23, 2022. https://en.wikipedia.org/wiki/Riverdance

27. Ruth Ward Heflin, *Glory: Experiencing the Atmosphere of Heaven* (McDougal Publishing; 5th edition, August 23, 1996).

28. Theresa Dedmon, *Born to Create: Stepping into Your Supernatural Destiny* (Destiny Image Publishers, April 1, 2012).

29. Graham Cooke, *Crafted Prayer: The Joy of Always Getting Your Prayers Answered* (Sovereign World Ltd., January 1, 2003).

30. Theresa Dedmon, Born to Create: *Stepping into Your Supernatural Destiny* (Destiny Image Publishers, April 1, 2012).

31. Nguyen, Thai. "10 Surprising Benefits You'll Get From Keeping a Journal." HuffPost.com. Accessed August 10, 2022. https://www.huffpost.com/entry/benefits-of-journaling_b_6648884

CHAPTER SEVEN

32. *Joan of Arc*, Christian Duguay (DIR), 1999, Movie Trailer, YouTube Video, 03:06. Accessed October 23, 2022. https://www.youtube.com/watch?v=6w0hUwBbtpc

33. Joan of Arc. AZQuotes.com. Accessed August 10, 2022. https://www.azquotes.com/quote/496497

34. Joan of Arc. AZQuotes.com. Accessed August 10, 2022. https://www.azquotes.com/quote/1398128

35. Michelangelo. AZQuotes.com. Accessed August 10, 2022. https://www.azquotes.com/quote/1042539

36. Christ John Otto, *An Army Arising: Why Artists are on the Frontline of the Next Move of God* (Belonging House Creative, October 16, 2013).

37. Dedmon, Theresa. Create Without Walls E-Course. Accessed October 23, 2022. https://learn.theresadedmon.com/

CHAPTER EIGHT

38. Scott, Ridley. *Gladiator.* United States: DreamWorks Distribution, 2000, YouTube Video, 02.06. Accessed October 23, 2022. https://www.youtube.com/watch?v=kfnvyGftvTQ

39. Steven Pressfield, *The War of Art: Break Through the Blocks and Win Your Inner Creative Battles* (Black Irish Entertainment LLC; 47716th edition, November 11, 2012).

40. John Cook. *The Book of Positive Quotations.* (Fairview Press; 2nd edition, September 10, 2007).

41. Christ John Otto, *An Army Arising: Why Artists are on the Frontline of the Next Move of God* (Belonging House Creative, October 16, 2013).

42. Van Gogh, Vincent. AZQuotes.com. Accessed August 10, 2022. https://www.azquotes.com/quote/112039

43. Matheson, George. AZQuotes.com. Accessed August 10, 2022. https://www.azquotes.com/quote/586356

CHAPTER NINE

44. Wonder Woman. IMDB.com. Accessed August 10, 2022. https://www.imdb.com/title/tt0451279/quotes/qt3429915

45. Jenkins, Patty. *Wonder Woman 1984*. United States: Warner Bros, 2020, YouTube Video, 03:55. Accessed October 23, 2022. https://www.youtube.com/watch?v=rAVVU9a9Kmk

46. Laurie Beth Jones, *The Path: Creating Your Mission Statement for Work and for Life*, (Hyperion - Acquired Assets, August 19, 1998).

47. Ibid. (pg 11).

48. Terri Savelle Foy, *Dream it. Pin it. Live it. Making Vision Boards Work for You* (Terri Savelle-Foy Ministries, September 21, 2015).

49. Ruth Ward Heflin, *Glory: Experiencing the Atmosphere of Heaven* (McDougal Publishing; 5th edition August 23, 1996).

50. David J Stanfield. *Wielding Banners: For Worship, Warfare and Ministry: The Who, What, Why and How of Banners in the Hands of Christians* (Out of Our Minds Banners, December 1, 2007).

51. Joan of Arc. BrainyQuote.com. Accessed August 10, 2022. https://www.brainyquote.com/quotes/joan_of_arc_193094

52. Michelangelo. AZQuotes.com. Accessed August 10, 2022. https://www.azquotes.com/quote/574899

CHAPTER TEN

53. Charles R. Solomon, *Handbook to Happiness* (Tyndale House Publishers, Inc.; Revised edition, November 1, 1999).

54. Michelangelo. AZQuotes.com. Accessed August 10, 2022. https://www.azquotes.com/quote/198606

55. Theresa Dedmon, *Born to Create: Stepping Into Your Supernatural Destiny* (Destiny Image Publishers, April 1, 2012).

56. Wallace, Randall. *Secretariat*. United States: Walt Disney Studios Motion Pictures, 2010, YouTube Video, 01.20.

Accessed November 5, 2022.
https://www.youtube.com/watch?v=C7RZdt77s9k

APPENDIX

RESOURCES:

CHAPTER SEVEN

Revival

QR Code #29 Sid Roth It's Supernatural
https://www.youtube.com/watch?v=Po8WPjPgRX4

Mario Murillo Hanford, CA Tent Meeting: PJ's Healing Word 2-22-22

"My dear in the red, with your hand right there, stand up, right now. Ever since that accident, your life has never been the same. And here's what's happening to you. Your bones, your nerves, your eyes, your skull, in this car accident. It was a massive injury to the head and a massive injury to your neck and the rest of your body. You shouldn't have survived. The car rolled and you should have been killed. How do I know that, by the power of the Holy Spirit.

You already feel different, your neck is healed in Jesus' Name. Amen. The compression in your lower spine is healed in the name of Jesus. Your legs are healed in the Name of Jesus. Whoo. You have trouble with pain and flexibility and it's all gone. Now, how would you like to insult the devil and glorify God? And move like you've once moved before, but I would like the church to give God the glory for this victory. Absolute miracle and I gotta tell you before you go now. I know, I just want you to stay right there, dear. What is your name? PJ. PJ, we'll go with PJ. There is a sport that you love and you had to give it up. It's back. God wants you to take it back up again and do it because you're going to have tremendous endurance, you had tremendous endurance and all that's coming back. What the devil stole because of that car accident. God has restored it. Somebody give God the glory!"

Https://www.facebook.com/mariomurilloministry/videos/947015709316960

Vessels of Fire and Glory by Mario Murillo

"All the electrifying adjectives in the dictionary shaken together, pressed down and running over will not begin to describe the soon-to-come, greatest outpouring of the Holy Spirit of all-times – what the Bible called 'the latter rain'. You are going to see lay members carry out an amazing ministry through gifts of the Holy Spirit. There will be wholesale cures of incurable conditions healings of the blind, deaf, dumb and handicapped, and creative miracles that will strain the imagination. For those born with-out eyes, ears, fingers, arms or legs – or those who have lost them through disease or accidents – God will make new ones. Many astonishing miracles will happen to bring on an International Christian breakthrough."

A.C. Valdez Azusa Street Revival

Tests You Can Take -

The Enneagram Personality Test. Truity.com. Accessed October 24, 2022. https://www.truity.com/test/enneagram-personality-test

16 Personalities. 16Personalities.com. Accessed October 24, 2022. https://www.16personalities.com/

Destiny Finder. DestinyFinder.com. Accessed October 24, 2022. https://destinyfinder.com/

Disc Profile. DiscProfile.com. Accessed October 24, 2022. https://www.discprofile.com/

Wired That Way. ThePersonalities.com. Accessed October 24, 2023. https://thepersonalities.com/

ABOUT THE AUTHOR

After crying out to God, PJ discovered a world she had never known before.

PJ's passion is to help others push past the resistance and apathy of life and discover their purpose and destiny. Through the arts she has found freedom for her soul!

As a lifelong learner and outdoor enthusiast, PJ found healing through her love of journaling, dance, and the arts.

Her family, friends, and faith are her greatest joy!

PJ has been mentored by Theresa Dedmon and is a graduate of Create Academy.

She is currently a Co-leader for Theresa's Create Forum and Focus Dance Group.

PJ offers:
Journaling Workshops and Retreats
Passionate Prayers and Declarations
Women of Courage Mentorship
www.DesertThunderArts.com

t